About Island Press

Since 1984, the nonprofit organization Island Press has been stimulating, shaping, and communicating ideas that are essential for solving environmental problems worldwide. With more than 1,000 titles in print and some 30 new releases each year, we are the nation's leading publisher on environmental issues. We identify innovative thinkers and emerging trends in the environmental field. We work with world-renowned experts and authors to develop cross-disciplinary solutions to environmental challenges.

Island Press designs and executes educational campaigns, in conjunction with our authors, to communicate their critical messages in print, in person, and online using the latest technologies, innovative programs, and the media. Our goal is to reach targeted audiences—scientists, policy makers, environmental advocates, urban planners, the media, and concerned citizens—with information that can be used to create the framework for long-term ecological health and human well-being.

Island Press gratefully acknowledges major support from The Bobolink Foundation, Caldera Foundation, The Curtis and Edith Munson Foundation, The Forrest C. and Frances H. Lattner Foundation, The JPB Foundation, The Kresge Foundation, The Summit Charitable Foundation, Inc., and many other generous organizations and individuals.

The opinions expressed in this book are those of the author(s) and do not necessarily reflect the views of our supporters.

Empathic Design

Empathic Design

PERSPECTIVES ON CREATING INCLUSIVE SPACES

Edited by
Elgin Cleckley

ISLANDPRESS | Washington | Covelo

Library of Congress Control Number: 2023937549

All Island Press books are printed on environmentally responsible materials.

Manufactured in the United States of America
10 9 8 7 6 5 4 3 2 1

Keywords: ally, belonging, citizen expert, colonialism, community process, design education, design justice, empathy, grief, healing, historical marker, memorial, memory, monument, park, patriarchy, public art, public space, racism

This project is supported by the National Endowment for the Arts. To find out more about how National Endowment for the Arts grants impact individuals and communities, visit www.arts.gov.

Contents

Acknowledgments

THIS BOOK WOULD NOT BE POSSIBLE if not for the communities of care I've been so fortunate to be within.

First, I would like to thank Dean Malo Hutson for his constant support of this project and for sustaining our University of Virginia community with empathy and determined care. As an alumnus of the school, I am honored to serve with such committed students, staff, faculty, and alumni.

I greatly thank Jeana Ripple, chair of the University of Virginia's School of Architecture, and Associate Professor Barbara Brown Wilson of UVA's Equity Center and School of Urban and Environmental Planning. Along with Professor Alissa Diamond of the University at Buffalo, your advice, guidance, and unwavering support have helped make this work possible—personally and professionally. Conversations with Garnette Cadogan of the Massachusetts Institute of Technology helped form early thoughts for this book.

I would also like to thank Professors Lucia Phinney, Lisa Reilly, Alison Booth, Sheila Crane, and Mona El Khafif. Thank you to Professor Ila Berman for her early insights expanding the foundations of my scholarship. Anselmo Canfora has been a constant link to this work over decades, helping it become what it is.

_mpathic design seminars, courses, and design studios at the University of Virginia School of Architecture since 2016 provided spaces of trust with dedicated students to explore the methods, processes, and approaches.

An enormous thank-you to Lauren Brown, Gabriel Andrade, Omer Gorashi, Michelle Tran, Nicole Starego, Sam Ashkani, Abdureuf Hussien, My-Anh Nguyen, Mira Davis, and Jaeger Lajewski. These designers, historians, and place-makers influenced the mission and vision of this book, and I am excited to see how they will improve our communities and the built environment.

Ideas for this book began in 1995, when I was a graduate student at Princeton University, in a thesis with Thomas Leeser. I thank Princeton for the space to explore what is now a reality and for the feedback from Sylvia Lavin and Fran Lebowitz.

My time in Toronto was a colossal imprint. I thank colleagues from my time at the Ontario Science Centre—Jennifer Martin, Julie Bowen, Mary Jane Conboy, Karen Hager, Vishnu Ramcharan, Cathie Spencer, Julie Jones, Aylin Doyle, Rich Vieira, Niina Gates-Kass, Ken Locke, Gus Dassios, Bhavleen Kaur, Bernie Hillar, Donna Francis, Dawn Lee, Hooley McLaughlin, Denise Frechette, and Walter Stoddard. Many thanks to my extended Toronto friends for all of your support over the years: Carmelo Millimaci, Joe Comeau, Kimberly Gartner, Colin Ripley, and Jaime Aitken. Thank you to Monica Vaca-Evan and Aaron Evan.

Presentations at Harvard University; the Rhode Island School of Design; MIT; the National Maritime Museum in Greenwich, London;

Hampton University; Carleton University; the University of California, Berkeley; the University of Texas at Austin; and Toronto Metropolitan University influenced this book. Thank you to MacDowell and Loghaven (Sarah Swinford and Lynne Ghenov) for your support and to the Design Futures Forum.

I thank Heather Boyer and Island Press for their impeccable guidance and support. It is an honor to be in the incredible company of dedicated designers, and I thank the contributors for their essays, thoughts, conversations, and friendship.

My parents, Mr. and Mrs. Eugene and Louise Cleckley, provided the essential foundations to see the world through empathic eyes, and I am forever grateful. My brothers, Eulois and Gene, operate in the portal you opened for us—supporting every page of this book.

Introduction

Elgin Cleckley

On July 12, 1898, in Charlottesville, Virginia, on what we can assume was a sweltering summer day, John Henry James, a Black ice-cream salesman, was lynched. James was falsely accused of assaulting a White woman, Julia Hotopp, at a homestead built on a former plantation just north of downtown. On that site today you'll find the city's largest park, Pen Park, which you can visit and never know of this story. James was lynched just west of town, off Route 250 at what was once Wood's Crossing, just where the rolling hills begin on the drive to the Blue Ridge Mountains. There is no way to know exactly where Wood's Crossing is in the thick mass of tree growth just west of the entrance to the Farmington Country Club, since there is no historical marker. I drive past the site often, and it's always the same—I feel vibrations run through my body and must pay attention where the road starts to undulate as I head east, in the direction of Staunton, Virginia.

Staunton was where authorities were taking James (reportedly for his safety) to face a jury. He was taken off the train at Wood's Crossing by a horde of angry White men, who didn't bother to cover their faces, according to accounts.[1] James's body was shot by "twenty or thirty revolvers . . . with perhaps forty or fifty bullets."[2] Carl Hotopp, Julia's brother, arrived at Wood's and, according to accounts, "emptied his revolver in James's body." Pieces of James's clothes and body were kept as souvenirs.[3]

Figure I-1: According to Charlottesville historical researcher Jane Smith, Wood's Crossing, where John Henry James was lynched, is near the entrance to Farmington Country Club, Charlottesville. (Photo by Elgin Cleckley)

I often search in downtown Charlottesville to see if I can find the site of Dudley's bar on East Main Street, where I once lived. At Dudley's, James was arrested by authorities who determined that he "answer[ed] somewhat the description of Miss Hotopp's assailant," according to the *Charlottesville Daily Progress*.[4] No luck finding it yet—I keep looking for historical records and asking colleagues and community members to see if there are any hints of where Dudley's once was. One day I'll find it, given that the level of consciousness of doing the public work of uncovering and telling Black narratives here in this small city of just over forty-seven thousand is high.

Over 120 years later, the narrative of James's lynching finally became spatial in the city and county through the Albemarle County Office of Equity and Diversity (then led by Siri Russell) and the Community Remembrance Project, led by the Equal Justice Initiative (EJI) of Montgomery, Alabama. The project collaborates with communities "to memorialize documented victims of racial violence throughout history and foster meaningful dialogue about race and justice today"[5] with design interventions that EJI says concertize the experiences of racial terror—bringing forth untold narratives. One of these design interventions is EJI's Community Soil Collection Project—which in 2019 gathered soil at the site where James was lynched (shown in figure I-1) to add to the multicolored, granular memory wall holding row after row of soil from the 4,400 sites documented by EJI at the Legacy Museum in Montgomery, Alabama, the first stage of one's visit to the National Memorial for Peace and Justice. When I visited the Legacy Museum, I immediately recognized the red soil of Charlottesville in the glass jar holding James's name—the same color as the famous red brick of the Academical Village at the University of Virginia.

Empathy in Design

You should be yourself some of the time. You should be with people who are like you, who are facing what you're facing, who dream your dreams and fight your battles, who recognize you.

And then, other times, you should be like people unlike your-self. Because there is a problem as well with those who spend too little time being anyone else; it stunts the imagination in which empathy takes root, that empathy that is a capacity to shape-shift and roam out of your sole self.

—Rebecca Solnit, *Recollections of My Nonexistence*[6]

Sociologist and researcher Karla McLaren defines empathy as "a social and emotional skill that helps us feel and understand the emotions, circumstances, intentions, thoughts, and needs of others, such that we can offer sensitive, perceptive, and appropriate communication and support." McLaren also shares that empathy helps us engage with structures—"buildings, public spaces, and living and working areas."[7] McLaren's definition of empathy is one of the few I've found that takes us into a spatial understanding, and in my work, I add a Black lens to move beyond the co-opting of empathy, popularized by the business field as a scenario-building stage to consumer-focused design thinking. This is not a take on empathy that occupies, possesses, or extracts from the existence of another for gain.

I explore ways to activate the imagination to spatially see outside of myself, referring to Solnit's quote opening this section. I add to these definitions a cyclical understanding of time and place—moving, walking, exploring, and researching. This forces us to look outside ourselves to generational lived experience to deeply understand what to uncover and what can be translated into built form. I propose that if we explore, discover, and investigate empathically to reengage, as McLaren notes, we work our empathic muscles, becoming better designers and practitioners.

I believe that inclusive public space needs to be of two things: the first, care (based on empathic connection and support); and the second, space in the design process that seeks to understand and translate the past (and its foundation to the present) through designs that inform, exhibit, interpret, and educate. The result is inclusive public spaces with intersections of identity, culture, history, memory. The result is spaces that care for and support humanity.

Empathic design is part of the design justice movement. Designer Sasha Costanza-Chock explains, from the work of the Design Justice Network, that "design justice rethinks design processes, centers people who are normally marginalized by design, and uses collaborative, creative practices to address the deepest challenges our communities face."[8] Empathic design supports by recognizing that people are seen and acknowledged in public space through layers of identity, culture, history, and memory. It affirms that our layered emotional responses to places are both valid and complex and that in the built environment, form, symbol, material, and scale all play a role—ideally, one that culminates in deeper relationships with nature and the landscape. It says, "We are here," and, equally, "We see you."

Empathic Design Defined

In feedback from community members, I've learned that empathic design offers communities the opportunity to acknowledge the full history of a place and engage in a healing design process through planning for future uses that engage and embrace everyone in a community.[9] Here in Virginia, the wounds are deep and are seldom recognized or dealt with in a restorative way. There is more work to be done.[10] I believe that if we design with empathy, we can begin to rethink, rebuild, reckon, and reengage with public spaces that have untold narratives. Most often, especially here in the South, those untold narratives are Black, Native, or female.

Empathic designs push back on the historical and ideological approaches of designing public spaces exclusively for and by dominant narratives. In the words of architect and humanist Robert Lamb Hart, we "read relationships between buildings, landscapes, and streetscapes in social terms, too, imagining their dialogues and conflicts and sensing them rejecting or welcoming us, almost like a family member or friend."[11] Hart's words speak to me, taking me back to my first explorations in Charlottesville as an undergraduate student at the University of Virginia's School of Architecture, an empathic perspective on the discomfort I felt here then but requiring a lens of Black American lived experience. Empathic design requires a deeper sense of emotional response depending on who you are, who defines your community, and the history (seen and unseen) of the space.

EMPATHIC DESIGN

- recognizes how people are seen and acknowledged in spaces and the built environment through layers of identity, culture, history, memory, and place;
- culminates in deeper relationships with nature and the land;
- devises and develops designs that are a visual representation of inclusive imagination melding with emotion, resulting in a space that reestablishes trust through connective encounters;
- believes that design is iterative, changing, and shifting to say, "We see you," and "We are here";
- believes design works with and by the communities it affects;
- understands that marginalized lived experience holds deep memory, requiring designers to shift through time in their work to approach these memories with respect.

EMPATHIC DESIGNERS

- understand that the methods and approaches that create harmful designs can be retooled and rethought to produce designs that help, support, and bring community together;
- develop approaches and methods that respectfully acknowledge

often untold, marginalized narratives of the past, with goals of operating with care in the present, to create inclusive and equitable design futures;

- work co-creatively and facilitate spaces of trust in all stages of the design process, always honoring lived experience;
- redefine public space—working with nuance and meaning in material, reflection, respect, honor, and developing generational spaces for joy, their work generates meaning in form;
- work with care, bringing forth untold, marginalized voices into form, changing ideological or dominant narratives in the built environment;
- constantly self-analyze to work with care, always open to change to meet the needs of the communities in which they collaborate.

This Book

My design experience and my personal experience of spaces as a Black man offer but one perspective. In this volume, ten other designers and activists share their perspectives and their empathic design approaches and methods, modeling this design justice movement in practice. You will see that the agreements and different points of view feel like a community meeting. I believe that this is the spirit of co-creation our field so desperately requires.

The contributors all demonstrate how empathy plays out in their work and personal approaches.

Welcome to our time together.

CHAPTER 1

From Empathy to Ethics

Christine Gaspar

WHAT DOES IT MEAN TO HAVE AN ETHICAL DESIGN PRACTICE? In sixteen years of practicing community-engaged design in nonprofits that collaborate with marginalized communities, it's a question I've asked myself a lot. Even more than in conventional design studios, practices that directly involve communities affected by their work raise so many questions about power, responsibility, and what designers owe the people impacted by our work.

In his talk "When Design and Ethics Collide," George Aye of Greater Good Studio pointed out that "we lack an ethics-based framework for good design" and instead have proxies to guide us, which can make designers "quite dangerous."[1]

The idea that empathy should play a role in design—which over the past ten years has become a mainstream idea, alongside the rise of design thinking and human-centered design—has been one of those proxies for ethical practice. When empathy emerged, it was an important idea in design—one that questioned the historical relationship of design and power, saying it's not enough for those with money and power to hire designers to do their bidding and let those impacted by it live with the consequences. It asked designers to consider their "end users" in new ways and bring them into the conversation. In mainstream design practices, that's often driven by a profit motive—better product research leads to more money. But in community-engaged design, at least, considering end users' needs is central to the values that guide our work.

But how to do that? Many designers have used the empathy framing to identify meaningful ways to genuinely center communities in their work. But when we use empathy as a proxy for ethics, it seems to hold the potential to lead us somewhere meaningful but without the rigor to ensure we get there.

The Limits of Empathy

The core idea of empathy is "the ability to share someone else's feelings or experiences."[2] It's related to sympathy but differentiated in that "while *sympathy* is a feeling of sincere concern for someone who is experiencing something difficult or painful, *empathy* involves actively sharing in the emotional experience of the other person."[3] In design practice, "empathy" has come to mean the idea that we should incorporate the perspectives and lived experiences of our end users into the design of products, spaces, experiences, solutions, or whatever we are designing.

Melba Sullivan is a psychologist who led a clinic that provides support services to asylum seekers who have been tortured in their countries of origin. When I was collaborating with her organization on a guide to applying for asylum, she told me that understanding trauma and lived experiences in this kind of work is not about empathy "because you *don't* know their experience. And to think you do is narcissistic."[4] Though it's our responsibility to try to understand as much as possible, we also have to acknowledge the real limits of what we truly know about the experiences of others, particularly when our community of focus has experienced forms of oppression that we have not, but also in the more mundane ways that our biases limit our perspectives.

Another way the idea of empathy in design feels incomplete is that it's not clear how to use that understanding in the design work, leading many designers to believe that with only a few conversations, a focus group, and a journey map, they could speak for and design for their end users. Asking designers to rely on empathy is the equivalent of what George Aye calls the "BYOE, or bring your own ethics" approach to design, which he argues can lead to exploitation and concentration of power.[5] Focusing on a vague idea like empathy prevents us from naming something more substantial, such as making sure people who have lived experience or who are directly affected by a design project are fundamentally involved in the design process in meaningful ways.

So, What's the Alternative?

I'll start by saying I don't have the answer. But maybe empathy is taking us in the right direction—it holds an important idea about the relationship between designers and those affected by their work that we were missing before. It's suggesting something about how the designer shows up for this work and something about how that work is tied to the people affected.

As I've reflected on my own experiences, both successful and decidedly not, the pieces that have felt like they really grounded the work in meaningful ways are ones that are explicit about the relationship to the community and, increasingly, ones that delve into the work I have to do within myself to show up and hold space for the experiences and perspectives of others. Rather than empathy, I would call these two things accountability and compassion.

Accountability—How the Work Is Tied to the Community

Accountability more or less involves taking responsibility for a set of duties that we have to show we've followed through on, and for which failing to do so leads to some kind of consequences. In the talk mentioned earlier, George Aye argued for a code of ethics, standards of practice, and other tools that I would argue are all mechanisms for creating a clear chain of accountability between designers and the communities impacted by their work. Among other things, these can include guiding practices we use within our organizations, agreements we make directly with partners, external guiding practices we create with other practitioners in our field, and how we use evaluations and feedback to keep improving.

Consequences are an important part of accountability because no matter how well we do this work, we will get some things wrong. We should anticipate that we will make mistakes that cause harm and, obviously, try to prevent that from happening. But when we do cause harm, having consequences means taking responsibility for the impacts of our actions and being prepared to make amends.

Compassion—How We Show Up in Our Work

One of the things that draws us to empathy is the idea that there should be something going on internally for us as designers beyond just problem-solving. The empathy framework hints at some emotional labor in how we understand the experience of others and hold space for them.

I think compassion is really what we mean when we talk about empathy.

Compassion, as I've come to understand it through the writings of contemporary Buddhist practitioners Lama Rod Owens and Sharon

Salzberg, is the ability to recognize and actively show up for the pain and suffering of others, despite our own discomfort. It's different from empathy in that it does not require us to share the suffering of the other person, but instead to feel concern and care for them, and "motivation to improve the other's wellbeing" but with some perspective that allows us to show up and be helpful.[6] Compassion asks us to see what the person is feeling, to see their full humanity, including their strength and resilience, and to see our own role as standing alongside them to support them in ways that are appropriate and consensual.

What Does That Look Like in Practice?

What does it look like to be accountable to and compassionate toward the community your work is intended for?

There is no one answer, and in fact, the chapters in this volume speak to all the ways this work can be done. The ideas I share here draw significantly from my time at the Center for Urban Pedagogy (CUP) from 2009 to 2022 and at the Gulf Coast Community Design Studio (GCCDS) from 2006 to 2009, though I also reference some examples from other practices that I've found to be useful guideposts. They reflect some of the elements that I have found grounding in my work and that have felt like embodiments of the ideas of compassion and accountability. Below are brief introductions to the ways GCCDS and CUP work, and the subsequent section highlights some of their key practices.

The Resource Ally Model: CUP's Approach

The Center for Urban Pedagogy, based in New York City, is a nonprofit that partners with marginalized communities to create visual explanations of complex policy and social justice issues those communities are organizing around. CUP applies the "resource ally model" in its work, which centers the leadership of community organizing groups; these groups identify the issues and strategies for change they want to work on and then call on partners such as CUP to support that work when it advances their needs.

Most of CUP's projects are created through programs in which it hosts an open call for participation from community organizations and advocacy groups that want to create such materials as part of their organizing work. The work is driven by organizers and community members themselves and is a means to build power and advance self-determination. The projects help community members gain access to rights and public services and make their political voice heard.

CUP staff facilitate the collaborations, which are three-way partnerships of CUP, the community organization and its members, and a design team that creates all the visual content. CUP does extensive outreach to let organizations know they can apply and how to do so. Transparent criteria are shared publicly, as are the application questions. CUP also tries to build as much transparency as possible into the collaborations, detailing the roles of each participant in the project early on and sharing timelines and other relevant information.

CUP selects and pays leaders in the art and design worlds and organizing and advocacy worlds to be jurors who will select both the community partners and the designers who apply to collaborate on the projects. The jury process is seen as another way to be publicly accountable to the communities the work serves. CUP also sees the makeup of its staff, all of whom hold marginalized identities that overlap with the different communities the organization collaborates with, and the organization's board, as spaces to build in accountability in the form of representation of lived experiences that inform decisions about the organization's structure and programming.

The community organization brings directly affected individuals into the process at various points, either as part of the core team that comes to every meeting or at key moments in the design process. CUP pays community members a stipend for their participation, to ensure that they can participate and to value their lived experience as one of the critical expertises needed for the project.

Those expertises include helping the project team understand key information, such as what their perceptions, questions, and experiences are with the policy or system to be explained in the project; where they have experienced challenges in that system; and what kind of information they need now or would have wanted when interacting with the system. This helps the team shape the content of the project. The team also works with community members to understand how they want—and don't want—to be depicted in the projects. They talk about the language, visual directions, illustration styles, and other aspects of the design and content of the materials, what resonates with them, how it reads to them, and how to prevent perpetuating harmful stereotypes. Participants weigh in at different points during the development of the project and get to see how their input shapes the final product. Often, community members are also involved in using the final publication or distributing it to other community members.

CUP does not play the role of designer in these projects, leaving that to the skilled graphic design teams. Instead, CUP staff lead the creative process, create the text content, manage the overall project, and facilitate the entire process. CUP provides training to the design team on bringing a racial justice and equity lens into design methods. Design conversations take place with the whole team at the table, and CUP facilitates these conversations to ensure that everyone can comfortably participate and move the process forward.

The final product is then used by the partner organizations in their organizing work or is distributed by them and other partner organizations. Some projects have gone on to be adopted by city agencies as well. Many projects have led to organizing wins for their communities, several have led to actual policy changes, and all help communities better understand and navigate the systems that impact their lives.

To Be Useful: The GCCDS Approach

The Gulf Coast Community Design Studio is a nonprofit design studio on the Mississippi Gulf Coast that is also part of the architecture school at Mississippi State University. It was formed by David Perkes after Hurricane Katrina devastated the Mississippi communities along the Gulf Coast in 2005. The studio was based in East Biloxi when I was there, a historic area of the city located on a narrow peninsula whose population was predominantly Black and Vietnamese American families. Though it is part of the university, the studio is made up of a full-time staff of architects, urban planners, and landscape architects who live and work in the community. When asked what its mission is, Perkes always responded, "To be useful." This account of GCCDS is based on my experience there in 2006 through 2009; the studio's practices have continued to evolve over time, so my experiences may not reflect current practices.

The work of the studio grew organically over time through deep partnerships with locally led organizations. For many years, the design studio was housed within a larger Coordination Center where design services were provided alongside case management support for accessing benefits and rebuilding resources, volunteer construction teams, and a community group supporting the Vietnamese-speaking community. The center focused on serving multiple client needs, and design was only one piece of the puzzle, not the driver.

At GCCDS, our community members were largely low-income people of color whose homes had been damaged or destroyed by Hurricane Katrina. Community members opted in by coming to the shared space called the Coordination Center and meeting with caseworkers at the partner organization. Amid all the confusion, bureaucracy, and paperwork of disaster recovery, the center was a place where community members could talk to real people and get help in sorting things out. Once their case was processed, they would be introduced to the design studio, where one of our staff would work with them to design a new home that met their family needs, local updated building codes, elevation requirements post-Katrina, and any limitations related to the funding for the construction. Design staff also worked with the Coordination Center's construction managers and volunteer construction crews to make sure the home was built according to the approved plans.

Facilitating design conversations with community members took a lot of skill building for design staff. Clients were often reluctant to ask for too much or to make their needs known, both out of not wanting to seem ungrateful and simply from never having had the chance to genuinely have their needs met in this way before. The staff learned to support these conversations, working against the power differential and helping individuals feel safe stating their true needs, which often took extensive conversations both in the Coordination Center and in informal social settings such as porches and front yards.

Though most of the designers moved to Biloxi to work at the studio and were not originally from the area, their daily presence while living and working there connected them to the community. Individual home repair or rebuilding projects could take several months from the first meeting to move-in, and staff and residents would see each other regularly in the neighborhood even after the projects were completed. Seeing people living in their homes and what worked for them or didn't also created an important feedback loop and sense of accountability to community members.

Over time, the work of the studio also grew to include conceptual design work for local nonprofits and local government agencies; larger-scale community plans that gave residents being left out of more top-down planning efforts a voice in redevelopment conversations; research and development on how floodproof construction could be used in small-scale commercial buildings; and architecture studio courses exploring local bayous that ultimately led to a large-scale landscape project restoring a major wetland area in partnership with the local housing authority. The work has continued to evolve over time, always driven by the underlying commitment "to be useful."

Some Elements of an Ethical Practice

Though the two organizations are different in their sizes, locations, types of services provided, and organizational structures, both incorporate methods that hold them accountable to their communities. This section explores those and draws on related practices from other organizations and practitioners who are exploring what it means to shape an ethical practice.

They don't exactly fall into the two categories of accountability and compassion, and many factors overlap, but they're presented here in roughly those groupings, in an effort to flesh out what those qualities might mean in practice.

Accountability Practices

If accountability is how our work is tied to the communities it affects, accountability practices in community-engaged design are the ways in which we structure our work to ensure that it is explicitly bound to the needs of the communities we work with and that the communities have some control over it.

Decentering Design

Design is a specialized skill that not everyone has access to. That means it always creates a power differential between those who do and those who don't. We as designers make choices about where and in whose hands we place that power. There are many different ways to think about that power structure and where in the equation a designer is located.

In my experience with CUP and GCCDS, both organizations decentered the role of design and placed it alongside other participants in the process. This created accountability from the outset: instead of the design practice holding all the cards in the projects, impacted communities had a say in determining what the work was and how it was shaped.

At GCCDS, the design studio was embedded in and sat alongside other service providers. It was called on when its services were needed, so that design was not the driver of activity but a useful tool to meet community needs. This also allowed the work to change considerably over time as new needs emerged.

As mentioned earlier, CUP framed its work as using the resource ally model, which centers the work that organizers in marginalized communities are doing to identify their own needs and solutions. In this model, design service sits alongside as a resource to support that work when it's useful to meet the community's needs. A similar framing was used by Melba Sullivan in her work with asylum seekers, which she described as using "a compassionate conduit approach." She framed her relationship to her client as showing up in this way: "I see what you're going through. I see your resources. I give and take nothing from you. I am not saving you."[7]

THE AGENCY TO OPT IN (OR NOT)

Both GCCDS and CUP also decentered design and fostered accountability to communities by creating clear ways for partners to opt in to projects. Designers didn't generate the projects; they responded to community needs.

Clients came to GCCDS through the Coordination Center and accessed design services only if the services met their needs, they were eligible for the services, and they opted in.

CUP often used open calls for partners, doing extensive outreach to let organizations know about the services and selecting partners at specific times of the year. Organizations opted in by applying to participate in CUP's programs.

Opting in also extended to how participants in different efforts could choose whether to participate, when to do so, and what information to share. Public Policy Lab, a service design nonprofit that conducts research with marginalized communities as part of its work, has guidelines for how it solicits informed participant consent, leading with a series of questions that should inform those practices, including the following:[8]

- Are you offering participants fair compensation for their time?
- Are you conducting the consent process in plain language?
- Are you maximizing participants' control over their data?
- Have you been explicit about potential harms?

This framework suggests other guidelines we as community-engaged designers might build for our practices and share with the communities we partner with.

Who Is an Expert?

How are the perspectives, experiences, and voices of impacted communities included in the design process, from beginning to end, to ensure that, rather than our empathy for them, they have the agency and power to speak for themselves?

Both CUP and GCCDS valued lived experience as an important expertise in the design process. At GCCDS, residents didn't get pre-designed houses; they got ones that met their specific needs, which required them to be an active part of the design conversation. At CUP, both community organizers working on the issues and individuals with direct lived experience of them were key parts of the project teams and process. Working together to create the projects with those affected by them made it harder for designers to ignore their needs. It's still possible for designers to steamroll their partners, however, so this alone is not enough.

WHO MAKES DECISIONS?

CUP used juries of organizers and advocates to select projects they worked on, explicitly creating accountability to its constituent communities. This is another instance of direct experience and knowledge replacing the need for "empathy."

For projects that didn't rely on open calls and juries, such as when CUP was hired directly by a project partner for customized work, the organization used a rubric for evaluating the project to decide whether to take it on. The rubric included questions about who the project was with and for, what potential it had to cause harm, whether it was appropriately resourced, and other questions related to CUP's values.

Greater Good Studio in Chicago (where George Aye is one of the founding partners) also uses a rubric for evaluating potential projects, which staff refer to as their "gut check." It is another example of internal accountability structures designers might use and includes these questions:[9]

- How desired is this project from the perspective of the end users?
- How likely is this project to have a positive impact on the end users?
- What type(s) of positive impact might come about as a result of our work?
- What is the client's mission, and how does it relate to social equity?

WHO PAYS AND WHO GETS PAID?

Both CUP and GCCDS also fundraised for the work ahead of projects, so that when community partners did opt in, the resources were in place for the project to move forward and community members' time was not wasted. CUP also made a point of paying all participants in the projects, including designers and community members. These were ways of being accountable to what we asked partners to contribute to the projects, namely, time, energy, and knowledge.

Detaching who pays for the projects (usually government and foundation grants, in both GCCDS and CUP cases) from who the clients for the work are requires additional accountability. While this creates opportunities for groups and individuals to access design services who might not otherwise have been able to, it also means the design organizations need to make clear who they will accept funding from, how they will limit potential interference of the funders in the projects to ensure the centering of community needs, and how they will address the power differential created by being the ones bringing funding to the design project. Creating community advisory boards or other bodies that can help guide this work, as well as internal policies about funding ethics, can be some ways to make that accountability explicit.

TRANSPARENCY

Another way to maintain accountability is through clear communication and transparency. At CUP, for example, staff members tried to make the process and the expectations for all participants as clear as possible from the start. Project teams kicked off each project by discussing everyone's expectations and reviewing a written set of agreements that made all the roles clear.

In projects that collect personal stories or data from individuals, there should also be transparency about how that information will be used, and there should be a way to share that information back out with community members when possible so they can use it as well. Both Public Policy Lab's consent guidelines and the Design Justice Network

Principles address this issue. The latter, which were created by a broad group of practitioners and which suggest a framework for a community-engaged design code of ethics, also include sharing "design knowledge and tools with our communities," another way to build transparency into the design process as a whole.[10] CUP saw one of the products of its work as the increased capacity of community groups and individuals to participate in and lead design processes on their own in the future, another way to increase self-determination and community control.

CONDUCTING AND USING EVALUATIONS

Collecting and using the learnings from evaluations is another way to stay accountable to communities. If conducted well, it gives participants a chance to share their perspective and gives designers the chance to learn from their mistakes and build on their strengths.

At GCCDS, designers received feedback from community members in informal ways. At CUP, project evaluations were used to assess the successes and failures of project processes and their overall impacts. Staff met annually to review evaluation results for multiple projects and to identify ways to improve our methods in response. This also helped us to recognize and respond to changing conditions and emerging needs we might not otherwise have seen. Significant program changes were made from year to year and whole new programs and training initiatives created in response to partner feedback.

Compassion Practices

While accountability focuses on the more formal, structural ways we shape our collaborations and organizational practices, compassion practices focus more on the ways we show up as individuals in our interactions and how we build our capacity to be present with grace and understanding despite our own discomfort.

Building Relationships, Not Transactions

It probably goes without saying that an ethical practice is built on relationships rather than transactions. Both GCCDS and CUP built relationships with partners over time (though relationships did not all have the same level of depth and trust). GCCDS did so by being embedded in the community in which it practiced and by letting projects emerge over time in response to partner needs. CUP projects were developed through a slow and deeply collaborative process. Projects typically took several months to a year to complete, allowing time to build trust.

Facilitation

The overwhelming majority of CUP's work took place in the form of how staff facilitated project meetings and conversations. As at GCCDS, it takes careful facilitation to make everyone feel comfortable in a design conversation and to ensure that they can share their honest feedback. CUP staff spent a lot of time building their facilitation skills and learning tools such as how to use plain language instead of technical design terms; breaking design concepts down into component parts so people could feel more comfortable talking about things like colors or fonts rather than an overall design; and supporting both designers and community partners in conversations when there were disagreements about what was working.

Designers at both CUP and GCCDS had to learn these tools because they are not ones we learn in design education. Whereas design school trains us to share our ideas as the best possible solution and to try to convince others of the same, strong design collaborations require that we ask our partners what we missed, what we got wrong, what isn't working. This also means emphasizing that community members, not us, are the ones who hold that expertise, and that we really need their perspective to get the project right. This not only emphasizes the value of their knowledge but also explicitly grants them permission to share critiques, which might feel uncomfortable or overly critical to them at first.

TAKING CRITICISM

The flip side of that coin is that we as designers need to be able to show up in a supportive and receptive way for that criticism. Our brains are not wired for that! It's something that requires personal internal work as well as active practice. CUP created a training to help staff and the designers they partnered with to reflect on the ways they showed up in design conversations and to practice receiving difficult feedback. The training encouraged designers to start from an assumption that the critique is true and to practice scripts they might easily reach for when feeling defensive. For example, they might take a deep breath and ask for more time (maybe even until the next meeting) to reflect on the critique before responding.

Design education focuses so much on our egos, but collaborative design practices need us to show up as part of a team and bring deep compassion especially to the moments when we're feeling most misunderstood.

Internal work, such as a meditation practice, helps with this, but so does training about power, privilege, and how we are holding our own and others' identities in these spaces.

SELF-REFLECTION

As designers, we need to develop our ability to reflect on our own identities and lived experiences and how they inform our practices. This means being willing to look at our own marginalized and dominant identities and understanding where our privileges, our blind spots, and our own traumas show up in our work. If we're doing it right, it can be pretty painful and uncomfortable.

In addition to conducting regular racial justice and equity trainings for staff, CUP created a training for its design partners to reflect on their own power and privilege and how the biases of their own education and socialization impacted their design work.

UNDERSTANDING TRAUMA

Community-engaged design often takes place in partnership with individuals and communities who have experienced trauma, and we as humans may also be carrying our own experiences of trauma. To do this work well, we need to learn about the ways that trauma can manifest and how to engage in a collaborative process that is sensitive to its participants.

At CUP, staff received training from partners and hired trauma-informed design practitioners to train staff and design partners.

On a larger scale, the training helped us understand trauma responses when we saw them in our work and to learn how to make space for how they manifested, which could include anger being directed toward us, people raising seemingly unrelated issues, or our realizing we may have unintentionally triggered someone.

That awareness can also manifest in how we design the details of our engagements with community members, looking for opportunities to foster transparency and agency, from small things such as letting participants choose where to sit to giving participants control over what they choose to share and how their information is used, or using agendas to be transparent about what's happening when.

Conclusion

Empathy opened up an important conversation about how we as designers engaged with the people impacted by our work. But design as a field, and particularly community-engaged design, would benefit from our moving beyond these general proxies and creating more concrete ethical guidelines for our practice. Accountability and compassion, and the examples mentioned here, may be only a piece of that larger puzzle. I look forward to learning from and exploring those ideas with other practitioners as we move toward a more ethical practice.

CHAPTER 2

Making Space for Grief

Liz Ogbu

In many ways, architecture is a profession that has been the epitome of the dominant white patriarchy, from most of the celebrated starchitects to the all too frequent obsession with buildings that are better known for the beauty of the object than the quality of life that they enable. I'm Black and female; my existence is the exact opposite of that system. So perhaps it is no accident that as I've built my own path in this field, I've been committed to a design practice that is rooted in elevating the stories of those who have most often been neglected or silenced.[1]

I WROTE THIS TO WRITER ALLISON ARIEFF when she asked for my thoughts about being a female architect. I can't help but think of it as I pen this essay about empathic design. To me, empathy is about being in an intimate enough relationship with someone that I can hold meaningful space for their pain and their joys, their struggles and their hopes, while also maintaining a critical lens regarding how my own identity, experiences, and feelings are shaping the ways that I show up, am perceived, and have agency.

With that in mind, to write about empathy in my work is also to write about me in my work. Thus, this essay is part biography, part case study. It bridges two projects and two phases of my practice. And weaving in between these threads is a meditation on how being proximate to the ways in which we experience life means engaging with the ways place can serve as an armature for our pain, joys, struggles, and hopes.

A Space for Lost Stories

In 2012, I had just begun my consulting practice when Douglas Burnham, of the firm Envelope A+D, reached out about a potential collaboration. The local utility had issued a request for design teams to propose interim uses for its former power plant site in the Bayview Hunters Point neighborhood of San Francisco.

Back in the late 1990s, a community coalition led by mothers living in public housing on the hill above the plant fought for its closure. They were successful; the utility decommissioned the plant and tore it down in 2008. The utility cleaned the soil and capped it with asphalt, in part so that the clean soil wouldn't blow away while it figured out the long-term future of the site. The challenge was that the site was thirty acres, and because of various land use impediments such as overlapping leases, paper streets, and zoning restrictions, it was estimated that it would take at least ten years for any long-term redevelopment to occur.[2] Meaning that this community, which had already endured the power plant as a neighbor for decades, now had to contend with the equivalent of thirty asphalt football fields in their backyard for a decade more.

Recognizing that such a long vacancy could prove problematic, the company decided to make the site available for temporary activation. To put things in context, "temporary activation"[3] was in its initial heyday as people sought to creatively provide responsive solutions to underutilized properties, from parking spaces turned into miniparks[4] to temporary plazas in underutilized intersections[5] to pop-up retail in vacant storefronts and lots.[6] The challenge was that these interventions rarely took place in neighborhoods like Bayview Hunters Point.

Located in the southeast of San Francisco, the Bayview—as it is commonly called—has been a historically working-class and predominantly African American neighborhood with a rich cultural history. But it also exemplifies what the lack of spatial justice looks like. ("Spatial justice" is a term coined by geographers.[7] It means that justice has a geography and that access to resources, opportunities, and outcomes should be a basic human right.) The Bayview is home to much of the city's industrial uses, rampant disinvestment, and highest unemployment. All this in a city where the pre-pandemic median home price was well over $1.5 million,[8] which was twenty times more than the annual median income in this neighborhood.[9]

As someone who had frequented interim use projects elsewhere, I was also keenly aware that the consumers of many projects often didn't look like me or the people in the Bayview. And the projects often popped up quickly and with little community input (the fact that they were done with the intention of benefiting the community was supposed to be sufficient). So as Envelope A+D, the local landscape architecture firm RHAA, and I crafted our proposal, we felt compelled by these realities as well as the fact that the community had fought for this land. What happened here should respond to their needs and support a long-term vision connected to their hopes. We won the commission and began working to understand those needs and hopes.

Like many historically marginalized neighborhoods, the Bayview had no shortage of redevelopment plans sitting on a shelf or studies by city agencies, local universities, and nonprofits articulating the levels of need. But too often that kind of data tell a surface-level story far removed from the lived experiences that generated them. It also would have been easy for me to let my work and personal experiences be a proxy. After all, I had several years of experience working in similar communities and growing up across the bay in Oakland; I had some experience of what it meant to be Black in a city that was rapidly gentrifying and looking less like me. But while my skin color, proximity, and experiences gave me certain insights, these could never be a replacement for the voices and stories of those who called that neighborhood home.

In *Spatial Agency: Other Ways of Doing Architecture*, authors Nishat

Awan, Tatjana Schneider, and Jeremy Till talk about the concepts of "expert citizen" and "citizen expert."[10] An expert citizen is someone like me, a person with knowledge of space gained from professional training and experience and often possessing an agency derived from the power and privilege that knowledge bestows.[11] The residents of the Bayview are citizen experts, people whose knowledge of a place is born of the intimacy of their lived experience of that place. We often think of expertise as pure, objective. But the reality is that we are all humans, shaped by the experiences that framed our lives up until this moment. When we ignore or dismiss the way that our experiences influence the way we show up, we can become instruments of the very harm that we're seeking to alleviate. Pairing "expert" with "citizen" marries the subjectivity inherent in our humanity with the skills of practice. Conversely, "citizen expert" feels like a reminder that regardless of my years of experience, the true experts of a particular place are those who must navigate the intricacies of how that space works every day. Awan, Schneider, and Till make the case that to create spaces that add social value, the expert citizen and the citizen expert must come together in an exchange of mutual knowledge. Too often, space is not held for citizen experts to see or provide their knowledge as expertise. Part of the expert citizens' role can be to leverage their power and privilege to enable the conditions for that to occur and to foster a mutual expertise framework.

Here in the Bayview, we sought to lay the foundation of that framework. I led the design of the community process. I deliberately eschewed community meetings. Community meetings are often highly transactional platforms known more for people talking past—rather than with—one another. Creating the conditions for mutual knowledge requires building relationships. And building relationships requires building trust. We began our relationship building with a listening tour, meeting individually with activists who had fought for the plant's closure and cleanup.

Being willing to listen created an invitation for people to share their stories. Often, the stories were about the past; there was pride in what had been accomplished and lament that their stories had seldom been acknowledged or celebrated outside of the neighborhood. Now, as people were dying (from illness or old age) or moving away (through displacement or voluntarily relocation), stories were being lost. While these activists appreciated that we listened to their stories, they were skeptical that our work would yield anything but talk and plans that would never make it off paper. Not only had they been living with the conditions of spatial injustice for decades; they had also lived through other efforts to do good here. And too often, the commitments made, whether for new physical spaces or community benefits, ended up being shallow promises that were insufficiently met.

We walked away from those conversations knowing that it was not enough to sit and listen to their stories. We had to respond *tangibly* to show that we had *heard* them. We were struck by the repeated refrain of "stories being lost." We decided to reach out to StoryCorps, the national storytelling project. Every StoryCorps story is permanently archived in the Library of Congress. A long-term StoryCorps booth was at a museum in downtown San Francisco, but few stories from this neighborhood had been recorded. The organization had a mobile community recording program, so we offered to build a listening booth on the site to record stories.

We secured a shipping container and hired two community members and some local youths to help us trick it out to look like the interior of a grandmother's living room. We then offered the space to activists with whom we had met, as well as to the youth builders. We didn't place any requirements for the stories shared; we simply offered it as a space to tell the stories that they wanted preserved. After several recording days, we edited the stories into shortened clips, much like what you hear on NPR (National Public Radio) every Friday morning, and held a listening party.

Brené Brown has said that "stories are data with a soul."[12] The stories that emerged from that booth were soulful. In them, we heard the nuances behind the neighborhood statistics and the hopes that lay beyond the needs. At the party, many commented that none of this had been what they asked us for, but it was what they wanted. We had "heard" them. It opened the door to one of the best community conversations I've ever experienced. Ideas started flowing about what people wanted to see in the space in the short and long terms. And from that, the program of NOW Hunters Point was born.

NOW Hunters Point became a decade-long activation program on the power plant site. My team and I collaborated with those activists, community organizations, and the utility to create varied events that transformed the asphalt in ways that spoke to those needs and dreams. Programs ranged from job training workshops to movie nights to even an annual circus. During the pandemic, we leveraged our resources and network to make the site a food access point, giving away hundreds of bags of food monthly, and a COVID-19 testing location. Over the course of the program, more than thirty thousand people came and did something on the site that we hope transformed their relationship with the land.

These events were also our "community meetings." Beyond being transactional, community meetings often reward those who are "time rich" and exclude those who are "time poor." Many of our core constituents were time poor, working low-wage jobs with uneven or inconvenient hours. The traditional meeting model, in which we ask people to show up at the end of a nine-to-five workday to talk about a project that might not see the light of day for years, doesn't work for the time poor. That model is more about fulfilling the designer's need for community engagement and rewarding those whose power and privilege afford them the time and agency to participate in such processes.

Empathy here meant understanding how to create the conditions

Figure 2-1: One of the most successful events at NOW Hunters Point was the annual neighborhood circus festival, which we hosted in collaboration with the Bayview Opera House, Circus Bella, and Prescott Circus Theatre. It often attracted a diverse crowd of well over a thousand people from within the neighborhood and beyond. And it is an example of how joy was a key programming element. (Credit: Anne Hamersky)

that support those who are time poor to participate in this process of visioning and creation. A summer camp for youths, a family circus, a health access fair. These were activities that those who were time poor could afford and *wanted* to participate in. At every event, we had an engagement station where we could engage people about their needs and desires for the site. Knowing that different people (be they adults or children) have different ways in which they like to communicate, we offered multiple ways for people to share input, from surveys to desire cards to drawing prompts. I analyzed all the data collected, and we published an interim report in 2017 and a final report in 2022 documenting what we had heard and learned.[13] The purpose of the reports was to support trust building through transparency. We also weren't sure of

I WOULD LOVE A PLACE TO...
meet other youth that
want make a change in the
community & become
successful!

Figure 2-2: Engaging young people was a key imperative of our programming, and we ran many youth-specific workshops and engagement activities over the years. Some were for younger kids; others were for teenagers. Desire cards is a tool I created, inspired by the work of Tiny WPA and Candy Chang. I often use them to frame simple but illuminating open-ended prompts that can be platforms for deeper conversations. (Credit: Anne Hamersky)

the utility company's long-term plans and wanted to make sure that our other client, the community, had access to the data too.

Each year, additions and adjustments to the interim programming served as tangible responses to what we heard and saw from residents. We also used this platform to advance the design of the only permanent piece of redevelopment that has been able to move forward: a linear shoreline park on the edge of the site that opened in 2017. Beyond significantly raising the bar for the beauty and quality of public space in this neighborhood, the park, Hunters Point Shoreline, offered a permanent response to that lament of stories being lost. We designed the landscape to permanently ensconce the stories through elements such as quotes embedded in the concrete benches and interpretative signage that tells various parts of the neighborhood's history.

NOW Hunters Point was the first project of my solo practice. It offered an opportunity to build upon my experiences to date, and it felt like a success: attendance to and positive feedback from the events continued to increase, more community groups approached about partnering, and it inspired other projects within the neighborhood and within my practice. But not long after the park's completion, the project (and my practice) hit an important pivot point.

The Roar of Unprocessed Grief

The utility company began to think more concretely about long-term redevelopment. It hired a different design team to work on it but asked whether I would join as a consultant to bridge the two efforts. While the interim use work to date provided a strong baseline regarding community needs and desires, this new effort was complicated by the fact that it was led by a different team within the company, one whose practices were less aligned with the interim use effort.

Against my advice, the decision was made to start engagement with a traditional community meeting. It was the worst community meeting that I've ever been a part of. Residents expressed a lot of anger. They worried that if the site was sold to a developer, it would mean luxury condos and displacement. They were also upset with the city. After experiencing decades of disinvestment, they questioned why more hadn't been done to bring jobs and resources here.

That anger was important. Sometimes there's a tendency to dismiss the anger we see in places like this as the words of a few agitators. While some may use these situations as platforms, that doesn't negate the validity of that anger. The anger is often born of people's experience of not having their voices listened to in the past and their uncertainty about whether this will be the only time they'll get to speak their piece. That anger, as poet nayyirah waheed has so eloquently written, was "grief that has been silent for too long."[14]

What I saw from those neighborhood residents was a long trail of grief. It rocked me. For all the impact that the interim use had made and the praise we had received, I had never intentionally and directly addressed that grief. And yet, in that moment I realized that it had always been there, waiting beneath the surface for its moment to come out into the light. In my many years of community-engaged design work, grief had never been a part of the conversation. And as much as I had been a leader in redefining the field, I couldn't help but feel that I had been missing something fundamental.

It was clear that the structure for the long-term process was incompatible with my way of practice, so I exited it and refocused solely on interim use. For the first few months after the meeting, I was still in shock, unsure whether what had felt like great work before was still great if it didn't accommodate the grief. Amid this soul-searching, I received an invitation to give a TED talk. I used it to process this experience and what it meant for my work. I realized that the discovery of this grief didn't negate what had been accomplished; it merely illuminated what had yet to be tackled. I also realized that the first step in healing is acknowledging the pain, and as I looked back to the early work with StoryCorps, I saw the beginnings of an effort to do that. If anything, we needed more moments for that kind of listening and reflecting.

The following year, in 2019, the opportunity came to partner with artist Chris Johnson, who had created the *Question Bridge: Black Males* project.[15] *Question Bridge* was a groundbreaking video installation that transformed interviews with hundreds of Black men into a profound conversation about race and identity. We partnered with him to do *Question Bridge: Bayview*, a season-long conversation on race, identity, belonging, and space that culminated with a half-day symposium that October bringing together local residents, artists, nonprofit leaders, and activists in a conversation about how those issues play out in the neighborhood.[16] That thread continued with the event that concluded the ten-year interim use program: *An Intentional Shift*. Funded by the Kenneth Rainin Foundation and in collaboration with Bay Area choreographer Kristin Damrow and her dance company (KDC), Bayview girl dance troupe Feline Finesse, and Bayview artist Malik Seneferu, we facilitated a multimonth community conversation that culminated in a dance performance, art installation, and storytelling event that used the linear park as the stage and wove a story that explored people's grief and joy for the land and neighborhood.

Figure 2-3: Collaborating with local groups was a core part of our ethos at NOW Hunters Point, so we felt it was fundamental that neighborhood artists be a core part of our intentional ending. One of our artist collaborators was Lilla Pitman, the innovative coach and choreographer of the dynamic girl dance troupe Feline Finesse. As part of the final event, they performed a routine that centered vibrant cultural storytelling. (Credit: Amani Wade)

By the time the project ended, we hadn't healed the wounds. It took generations to cause them; it will take generations to heal them. But I hope that by not running away from grief and making space for it to exist alongside the moments of joy and hope that we continued to nurture, NOW Hunters Point was able to play a part in supporting the community on that longer healing journey.

The Highway to Nowhere

Awakening to grief in the Bayview ushered in a larger personal and professional process of embracing grief. I nerded out on conversations that centered it. I consumed books on trauma. I took trainings in somatics. I began to engage with my own unprocessed grief. And I took advantage of opportunities to make space for grief in my projects.

In the summer of 2020, I was approached by the City of Akron, Ohio. A deputy mayor had heard me give a talk about my work in the Bayview and the explorations in holding space for grief and healing. He believed that kind of process was needed for the Innerbelt.

The Innerbelt is an eight-mile highway that runs alongside Akron's downtown. In an all-too-familiar story in this country, its construction destroyed a thriving Black neighborhood, displacing over a thousand families and businesses[17] and decimating the economic base and social connections of those who lived adjacent to the site. Sometimes referred to as the "highway to nowhere," the project was halted because the state ran out of money to complete it nearly twenty years after its construction began. In 2018, the state vacated a portion of the highway and sold the land to the city. The decommissioned thirty acres had sat vacant since then. Now the city was ready to move forward with a process to identify potential future uses.

The Innerbelt offered an opportunity that hadn't been possible with NOW Hunters Point: a way to create conditions to hold space for grief

Figure 2-4: Located adjacent to downtown Akron, Ohio, the decommissioned portion of the "highway to nowhere" is a striking image in the urban landscape. And as this view from the Center Street Bridge shows, the highway not only displaced a community; it also viscerally divided neighborhoods. (Credit: Liz Ogbu/Studio O)

from the beginning. I'd never been to Akron before, but I sensed that there might be a lot of unresolved grief. So one of my first steps was to create an advisory group made up of stakeholders representing a spectrum of Akron residents. Nearly half are former residents of the destroyed neighborhood.

The advisory group, which began meeting virtually in early 2021, isn't a decision-making body but rather a group that provides feedback on the process and advises on opportunities for engagement and conversation. This group of citizen experts has been an important touch point both in learning about Akron and its history and in understanding the grief and advancing the healing that is needed.

Our society often teaches us to run from grief. As a result, we often don't have good individual or collective practices for holding grief—let alone processing it. Community meetings, as the Bayview project demonstrated, can too often be a place where grief explodes. Nothing is processed, and people are often left feeling even more raw. The advisory group in Akron has been an exercise in building an intentional community engaged in a brave space[18] that can hold the grief. We witness this whenever a sensitive topic arises in the meetings. Rather than letting it escalate, I deploy practices from the world of trauma recovery and somatic facilitation, such as slowing the pace of the conversation, isolating and unpacking the trigger point, and having people do exercises such as breathwork to help them return to their bodies. And recognizing that former residents often do more emotional labor in these conversations, I've started holding additional caucus meetings with them to provide them with space to unload and be held by those who have a more intimate understanding of their grief.

In June 2022, Akron was rocked by the horrific police killing of Jayland Walker. He was a young Black man who was killed as he ran away unarmed after a nighttime traffic stop. His body was riddled with over forty bullets. There were protests for days, and as I write this essay in early 2023, emotions are still raw. I realized that while the creation of the Innerbelt left a deep emotional wound for former residents, Jayland Walker's killing created a new one for so many others. In our first advisory group meeting after the shooting, I leaned deeply into the role of grief worker. I led with a guided meditation and then facilitated a heart-led conversation. It was a profoundly moving and emotional experience. And in the collective grieving of Jayland's death, we managed to find a greater collective holding of the grief about the Innerbelt.

The grief work at this level has not supplanted the larger engagement effort. After facilitating incubatory conversations within the advisory group for over a year, we started a broader engagement effort in the spring of 2022 involving focus groups with additional former residents, engagement pop-up stations at events across Akron, and activation events on the highway. We even collaborated with local nonprofits and the local paper to host a reunion event for former residents. As with the process in the Bayview, the power of story collecting and storytelling has been important here. Early on, it became clear how little known the story of the old neighborhood was beyond the Black community, something that clearly pains residents of that community and feels connected

Figure 2-5: As part of my work, I'm leading efforts to reconstruct the visual memory of what existed before the Innerbelt, including development of a more accurate map of the old neighborhood. We created a base map with generic landmarks and have been taking it to events that engage former residents, such as the one pictured here at the Innerbelt Reunion. While asking people to populate it with meaningful socioeconomic and cultural landmarks, we engage them in conversations about place-based stories and memories. It is a dynamic tool for both engagement and grief work. (Credit: Liz Ogbu/Studio O)

to ongoing challenges in the city. So as part of the project, I got an oral history initiative funded by a grant from Akron Civic Commons, a local place-based initiative that's part of a larger national public space campaign. We hired an interviewer, are recording the stories, and will be setting up a widely accessible digital collection at the public library. Grief pops up in some of these activities more than in others, but space for it is always held.

Holding grief in the process takes more time. We are just getting to the point where people are starting to articulate desires for the site's future, not just in terms of brick and mortar but also in what healing might feel like. Many have expressed that this is the first time they've participated in this kind of conversation in the city. And they have hope that it will offer a pathway not only to a better future for the Innerbelt but also to other efforts and relationships in Akron.

Embracing Grief

I began this essay by talking about what it means to be a Black woman in this field and how an understanding of myself informs my capacity for empathy. As these two projects have shown, one of the biggest areas of growth has been the ways I've learned to embrace grief as part of the practice. There is perhaps another essay to be written about what it means for Black women to be grief workers in a culture that has often looked to them to be the ultimate caretakers! And there are conversations to be had about the kind of personal supports needed to enable a person to show up as a grief worker (regardless of one's identity).[19] But for now, I will say that this grief work has made me more conscious and accountable to navigating the tension of empathy as a process through which I clearly see and hold space for both others and myself. And I hope that as my practice continues to evolve, I will be able to deepen my capacity to do this.

The work of supporting communities as they grieve, heal, and thrive is both a professional and a personal journey. The opportunity exists regardless of whether you're an architect, student, funder, nonprofit staff member, or community organizer or function in any number of community-engaged roles. The more comprehensive the grief worker framework, the more robust the community's grieving and repair work can be. Being a grief worker requires a willingness to take the leap and the capacity to do the work. As you think about your relationship with yourself, the communities you engage with, and the spaces you seek to transform, I hope it's a journey that you're open to taking.

CHAPTER 3

Unseen Dimensions of Public Space: Disrupting Colonial Narratives

Erin Genia

WHAT IS PUBLIC SPACE? It plays an essential role in the political and social life of America and occupies a revered place in our society's collective imagination. In the pluralistic United States, it's a site where people come together to work out pertinent democratic issues in a public setting. People depend on public space for leisure, for gatherings, and for acts of collective culture. It is a shared space of commonality. What are its meanings when people do not share culture or are oppressed by the existing legal and regulatory frameworks? It is experienced differently by people depending on where they fall in the socioeconomic hierarchy. While it can be a refuge for some, it is a place of danger for others. Indigenous people and people of color can be subjected to safety risks

---

The material in this chapter first appeared in the *Boston Art Review*, no. 4, August 16, 2019.

in public places, such as racial profiling by law enforcement personnel. Native women and girls can become targets for gender- and race-based violence. The utopian ideal of the public commons masks its origins as a product of genocide and ongoing settler occupation.

As a creative practitioner working in the public realm, I grapple with the disconnection between narratives surrounding public space and my reality as an Indigenous Dakota artist. In the Boston area and in other places around our country, these narratives are founded on principles that stem from settler colonial notions of landownership. Monuments and public art celebrating Boston's colonial history cover up and justify the reality that all land in America, public and private, has been stolen from Indigenous nations, using ethnic cleansing as a strategy for establishing this country. Without questioning these dimensions of public spaces and understanding the immense implications of this legacy, the artwork that inhabits it erases Indigenous peoples' historical and contemporary presence on the land.

How can people interested in public art think critically about this legacy to make work that addresses these complexities and to disrupt the disparities created by it? What role can artists working in the public sphere—architects building infrastructure in sensitive places, landscape architects contributing to ecosystems, media artists creating public interfaces, urban planners, and others—play in acknowledging the history of place? What methods can we use to create urban areas, monuments, art, and built environments that are responsive to these issues?

Public Space as a Settler Colonial Concept

The concept of public space, as currently understood in the United States, is aligned with outmoded values of institutions steeped in cultural supremacy and American exceptionalism. That vast cities and towns existed all over the continent prior to colonization contradicts the mythos that America was an empty and wild land with a few scattered uncivilized and primitive tribes. To get a sense of the vastness and great diversity of people whose societies were targeted for erasure, consider that there are now over 570 federally recognized self-governing tribes in the United States.

The traditional economies of Indigenous peoples across the land, which were based on ecological continuity, were destroyed through settler colonization, forcing dependence on capitalist economic institutions and welfare. Tribal homes in villages and towns, roads and highways, sacred spaces, and hunting and harvesting territories were co-opted and built over. This was made possible by corrupt legal practices that provided cover for land grabs for private landownership, military bases, national parks, railroads, and agricultural, mining, manufacturing, and forestry industries. American treaty responsibilities to tribes, which are supposed to be the law of the land, have been marginalized and minimized. Knowledge of this history, which undergirds today's political, social, and economic realities, is largely unknown. The lack of public education about it creates generational public ignorance.

Before colonization, Dakota people governed our land through intrinsic epistemologies of land and space, property, kinship, and relationship. The passage of the Dawes General Allotment Act of 1887 divided land held collectively by tribes into square plots of acreage deeded to individuals, with the remaining acreage sold to settlers for a pittance. This era ushered in the period of coercive assimilation that included the catastrophic boarding school system. Christian reformers were among the main advocates of assimilation and allotment, which were "intended to force the tribes into an Anglo-American system of tenure and inheritance, which they believed would quickly assimilate the Indians," because "communal landholding hindered the Indians' progress toward 'civilization.'"[1] Through communal living, traditional religious and social practices were preserved; after allotment, tight-knit communities were undermined and even destroyed. This forced assimilation of Indigenous people remains a powerful memory and a strong presence that colors how we perceive and experience public space. Where the land is carved up by private property, the dramatically altered landscapes and ecosystems, cities and roads, buildings, place-names, and other infrastructure reinforce Western domination over Indigenous peoples for everyone to see.

Figure 3-1: Lillian Pitt, *Welcome Gate at the Confluence Land Bridge in Vancouver, Washington.* (Photo courtesy of Confluence)

This power imbalance is palpable in the public sphere. Monuments, memorials, and public art that people interact with on a regular basis shape perspectives by presenting to the public an erroneous, incomplete, romanticized, tragic, offensive, or no image of Native Americans. This influences how tribal people are seen not only in society at large but inevitably also in public opinion. Public opinion leads to policy. The results of applying policy solutions based upon public opinion that has been tainted by misinformation have been devastating for tribes. A correlation exists between the level of public ignorance about Native Americans and the extent to which the dominant society is willing to exploit tribal people. Public ignorance about Indigenous people and a willingness to cast them as "other" has fueled the process of colonization and today paves the way for continued colonialist attitudes that are present in the popular discourses surrounding public space.

Indigenous Peoples' Presence

In the spring of 2019, I conducted a workshop called "Monuments in Perspective" for the MIT School of Architecture and Planning's 150th Anniversary "Experiments in Pedagogy" curriculum.[2] The purpose of the workshop was to probe hidden histories by highlighting the perspectives of Indigenous people. We considered questions such as the following: What pieces of human and natural history have been glorified or erased from a given location over time? What lies under a housing development, public park, parking lot, high-rise?

Over a weekend, we traveled to sites of significance to the Wampanoag, Nipmuc, and Massachusett peoples of this region. Tribal council member and culture-bearer Jonathan James-Perry (Aquinnah Wampanoag) led the group to several locations on Noepe/Martha's Vineyard, Manitouwattootan/Christiantown, and Aquinnah Cliffs and gave the group a tour of a traditional *wetu* house he built. He also led our group to Solstice Rock and Plymouth Rock. At each location, he shared significant history and facts about the site. Jean-Luc Pierite (Tunica-Biloxi), president of the North American Indian Center of Boston (NAICOB), read aloud the "1675 Order of Removal by the Massachusetts Bay Colony," which has had lasting impacts not only for tribal people of this region but for the settlement of America. He also discussed the work he is doing with NAICOB on repatriation and protection of local sacred sites.

"Monuments in Perspective" allowed our group to pursue an understanding of the land that is inclusive of the Indigenous peoples who live here and whose experiences are often erased. Critical discussion of historical legacies, public space, ethics of memory and the growing movement of colonial and Confederate monument removal, and questions of site specificity in public art and historic monuments took place.

Because of our unique location, history, and cultural and economic locus, how we express and disseminate ideas in the Boston region can have profound impacts on people in other places and spaces. As a result, our critical introspections and the actions we take on these issues must be reflective of the power of this place, and that begins with an understanding of the original peoples of this land.

Figure 3-2: Toma Villa, *She Who Watches*, 2019. (Photo by Woodrow Hunt, courtesy of Confluence)

Moving Forward

Public art, monuments, and historical markers that perpetuate defective views of Native American and Indigenous peoples are everywhere across America. Despite this reality, there is fertile ground for educating the public about Indigenous peoples through art and creating a strong Indigenous presence in these spaces that have historically excluded us.

Many movements within Western public art discourses have grappled with questions of monumentality and anti-monument status, memory, the confines of urban and architectural space, time-based public art production, performativity, and the environment. Little has been done to discuss the ways in which Indigenous peoples fit into these conversations.

One such endeavor is the Confluence Project, a public art effort spanning the length of the Columbia River, which divides the states of Washington and Oregon. Designed by Maya Lin, creator of the Vietnam Veterans Memorial in Washington, DC, its mission is to connect people to "the history, living cultures, and ecology of the Columbia River system through Indigenous voices."[3] The project has collaborated with local tribes and Indigenous artists to create site-specific pieces in six locations using sculpture, landscape art, architectural elements, and educational initiatives to draw attention to features of the land and its original inhabitants. The Confluence Project is a unique consortium of public, nonprofit, local, and tribal organizations working together to reflect the region's history, with Indigenous voices at the center. At the Vancouver land bridge location, artist Lillian Pitt (Warm Springs/Wasco) used petroglyph images to symbolize the site's ancestral memory and a large sculptural canoe paddle to show the connection between the tribal people of the place and the water. In May 2019, Toma Villa (Yakama) created a powerful performative piece depicting the ancient petroglyph image Tsagaglal/She Who Watches, at Columbia Hills State Park with a group of fourth graders who had taken part in a weeklong curriculum organized by the Confluence Project.[4] Efforts to honor the original peoples of the land, correct the lack of public education, and inspire awareness about these issues can be strategically addressed through collaboration and a mix of methods, with public art as a central force.

In rethinking public commons as sites for dealing with the legacy of colonization and the current realities of injustice, "the struggle to reclaim the commons should thus give way to a process of decolonization that transforms settler relationships with the land, Indigenous peoples and with each other."[5] Within this context, the ethics of public space is an urgent concern, and Indigenous peoples' perspectives must be respected and prioritized.

For Indigenous artists, working in the public realm is an opportunity to bring our distinctive worldviews to the forefront of discussions, which can have a wide impact on society. Interventions in the public arena by Indigenous artists create openings that can bring profound physical, psychological, and symbolic healing to colonized people and places.

In 2017, I was commissioned by the Seattle Office of Arts and Culture to produce a site-specific work at Seattle Center. My piece, *Resilience: Anpa O Wicahnpi*, also known as *Dakota Pride Banner*, was created to honor the many Indigenous people, living in diasporas, who left their reservations for cities such as Seattle during the Urban Indian Relocation Program in the mid-twentieth century. The banner is a celebration of diversity within our tribal communities and in all communities. It activated the space through color and light, paying homage to urban Native peoples' resilience through vibrant cultural expression.

Moving forward, some salient questions for consideration are as follows: In what ways can we decolonize places? How can we use social, political, and natural history to create space for justice? It is the responsibility of all practitioners working in the public sphere to address these

Figure 3-3: Erin Genia, *Resilience: Anpa O Wicahnpi* (*Dakota Pride Banner*), 2017. (Seattle Center; photo by Erin Genia)

issues in their works because they are fundamental to the land occupied, the resources used, the people and living things affected. Our communities must do more to support the work of Indigenous artists and practitioners of all kinds; respect local, regional, national, and international tribes' rights to self-determination and free prior informed consent; and learn about the importance of treaties. We must provide public opportunities to think deeply about our colonial past and present, to loosen the grip of our collective colonial approaches to the world, which continue to hold sway over our ideas and actions. Beginning with the land we live on, we can all contribute to work that tells history truthfully, acknowledges the legacy of colonization, honors the cultural significance of Native American communities, and considers the underlying ecology of place.

Figure 3-4: Erin Genia, *You Are On Native Land*, 2019. Digital montage.

CHAPTER 4

Renewing Spatial Agency for a Community: The Freedom Center, Oklahoma City

Cory Henry

I WAS INTRODUCED TO ARCHITECTURE through an interest in the arts and humanities. Thus, my interest in understanding cultures, experiences, perspectives, and behaviors and in improving the human condition—through empathic inquiry and critical analysis of contemporary conditions and challenges—is the method and purpose of my work. Design is the medium.

During the early part of my career, I was a junior architect at a firm that primarily worked on housing in underserved inner-city Black and Brown communities in Philadelphia. One such community is North Philadelphia. I was a new professional in the field, but through my background I could relate to the residents in whose lives and landscape we were planning to intervene by delivering new homes and public space to the broader community. During the design and program meetings, I was the only person in the room who reflected an understanding of the community, and the people and priorities at the table signaled that the texture and experience of daily life were secondary at best in decision-making on projects affecting working-class communities of color. It amounted to a kind of denial of my own reality.

The jarring effect that I felt then has proven productive as a foundational memory that has helped to guide my design and project principles since 2017 as the founder and principal of my practice, Atelier Cory Henry. I view my work as an aesthetic, social, and cultural construct that is derived from understanding the contextual conditions in which it is situated. My point of departure for any project is to engage the subject and communities with a humanistic perspective and an open mind.

In so doing, I have come to appreciate what can be spatialized and made part of a design and what cannot, and I often argue for facets of a project that may not be visible yet should rightfully be done. The approach has led me to projects that might seem to have little design promise, or to exist outside architecture altogether; but when these projects carry meaning to the communities whose needs and preferences they address, to engage them returns value to one's broader practice. Most of all, I have found, the way to understand a problem is to set aside the boundaries and mental trappings of architecture and simply listen and learn.

The Initial Process for the Freedom Center Project

A project that I am currently engaged with is the renovation of the Freedom Center of Oklahoma City, a modest one-level, 1,500-square-foot brick building in Northeast Oklahoma City. Atelier Cory Henry is leading the design of the renovation for a community-rooted nonprofit also named Freedom Center OKC (FCOKC) and in partnership with a local architect of record, Bockus Payne Architecture.

Figure 4-1: The deteriorated Freedom Center building. (Credit: Bockus Payne)

It is planned that the rehabilitation of the Freedom Center building will be part of a five-acre campus extending along three contiguous
blocks of Martin Luther King Avenue, to include a major new institution, the Clara Luper Civil Rights Center, funded by a city tax initiative called MAPS 4. The Freedom Center lot has been separated from
the larger MAPS 4 scheme and brought under the private control of
FCOKC, reducing the funding available to this component of the overall development but allowing for the Freedom Center's accelerated execution and community control via FCOKC. In its own words, FCOKC
is an organization established to educate, empower, and enlighten our
nation to reflect on the past, present, and future of the civil rights movement in Oklahoma. The center was established to continue the mission
of Clara Luper to "provide opportunities for deprived children to grow
up properly, to learn the value of self-help and to see the adult world

supported by a sense of belonging."[1] The board of directors of FCOKC includes former students of Clara Luper: Marilyn Luper Hildreth, Clara Luper's daughter; Leonard Benton, former chief executive officer of the Urban League of Oklahoma City; Judge Aletia Timmons; and other prominent agents of change in Oklahoma City.

Figure 4-2: Foreground: the granite civil rights monument, which honors local and national civil rights leaders, was gifted to Clara Luper and placed at the Freedom Center in 1992. Background: the deteriorated Freedom Center building. (Credit: Bockus Payne)

When FCOKC contacted me to lead the rehabilitation of the Freedom Center building, I hesitated at the outset, unsure what I might bring to what seemed to be a simple historical preservation project for a small, disused building. However, engaging with the community and FCOKC made clear to me the building's importance to the community in Oklahoma City and our national history—it is a historic landmark in its own right, having served as the home base for Clara Luper, an activist known as the "mother of the civil rights movement" in Oklahoma, and Oklahoma City's National Association for the Advancement of Colored People (NAACP) Youth Council. FCOKC's initial charge was to preserve the building as an important piece of Oklahoma City's history.

In initial conversations about the project with Marilyn Luper Hildreth, Leonard Benton, Christina L. Beatty (FCOKC project director), and Cecilia Robinson-Woods (superintendent of Millwood Public Schools in Oklahoma City), I stated that I was interested in the building not only as a symbol of the civil rights movement in Oklahoma but also for its history as a space and place of interaction, solace, and social experiences that will continue Clara Luper's work. To understand this, I needed to meet with community members and former students of Clara Luper. FCOKC was in the process of facilitating a series of community engagement events, which I then took part in, and had additional meetings that stemmed from these sessions. These meetings, both public and private, added layers of information to the research that we were doing. Stories from community members, former students of Clara Luper, and others influenced by her provided multigenerational perspectives and experiences.

This was a community living in constant disquiet as a result of the violent acts that were levied upon them daily. The building and its physical changes reflected the community's response to these atrocities. In its early stage, it was a repurposed gas station with windows and glass roll-up doors that not only filled the space with light but also created an interface with the spaces outside. It later became a windowless bunker because of the need to be safe from extreme hostility, rather than a place that reflected Clara Luper's mission and inclusionary beliefs. Photos of this rebuild show a white box with no windows. Some of the community members with whom I spoke remembered this iteration of the building. They also remembered the fear and concern that they had, simultaneous with the safety and hope that they had from one another. Unfortunately, this would be the state of the center for many years. Still, former students expressed that even with its enclosed nature, it remained a place of optimism and learning. They recalled how the bright glare of light filling the doorway felt like a portal to a world they would be better prepared to live in and change because of the lessons taught to them by Clara Luper and her partners at the Freedom Center. Thanks to these meetings, oral histories, and research, I began to think of the project in three parts: *the figure*, *the frame*, and *the field*.

The Figure, Clara Luper

Ms. Luper (1923–2011) may not have become well-known nationally among the pantheon of civil rights leaders. But in Oklahoma she was a towering figure, considered by many to be the mother of the movement in that state. She was an activist, arrested twenty times for peaceful protests. But she was also a determined educator and community leader for decades—a teacher in the Oklahoma City public schools and the host of a long-running community radio program, the *Clara Luper Radio Show*. She knew the importance of making sure that the operations of the oppressors did not become the system of reality and accepted by the Black community. As an example, she took her students to New York City via the northern route so that they could experience eating in desegregated restaurants. This undoubtedly amplified the resistance to racism and segregation within her students and others.

In 1958, Luper led a sit-in of fourteen members of the local NAACP Youth Council at the lunch counter of the Katz Drug Store, which refused to serve Black customers. The action lasted weeks and was ultimately successful: the company, a regional chain, integrated its stores not just in Oklahoma but also in Iowa, Kansas, and Missouri.

The Frame, the Building

In 1967, Ms. Luper organized the purchase of a former gas station in Northeast Oklahoma City, the historic heart of the city's Black community, businesses, and institutions. In accordance with its prior use, the building had wide windows and roll-down grates and sat on a paved plaza marked with traces of the fuel pumps. Clara Luper made the simple 1,500-square-foot rectangular building her headquarters, a place for community gatherings and youth education. She called it the Freedom Center.

I spoke with community members during engagement sessions and many one-on-one calls. Many in the community shared photos and oral histories of their experiences with Ms. Luper and at the Freedom Center building. Archival photos show Ms. Luper and her students in front of the roll-up doors of the gas station garages. I immediately thought of how they must have appropriated the building to their needs and interests, such as interfacing with the more public realm (streets, sidewalks) and showcasing the activities inside. Unfortunately, one year after the building was purchased, it was firebombed by the Ku Klux Klan. Undaunted, Ms. Luper and her associates rebuilt it through donations and labor support from the community, the NAACP, and others. It was rebuilt as a windowless structure for security.

While this hermetic structure would remain a safe space for the community, the site itself no longer performed as it likely did in its early form, which allowed activities from the inside to expand to the outside via the roll-up doors and relatively expansive windows. A photo from approximately 1992 shows Ms. Luper in front of the center in its last form. A gable roof had been added and red brick had been applied to its facades, except in the rear. The absence of brick on the rear facade was likely due to cost. Ms. Luper painted the interior floor red on one side and blue on the other. When I saw these photos, I immediately commented to FCOKC that "this was the first moment of agency over the aesthetic of the building that Clara Luper had." While racist violence caused the building to be fortified, it was clear that Ms. Luper wanted it to still have qualities of a home, a safe space, for those who were there. Thus, as we considered the era of restoration for the project, it was clear to me that the building should be restored to the brick and gabled roof version of itself.

Figure 4-3: Clara Luper standing in front of the Freedom Center, circa 1992. Behind her, and below the building sign, are small commemorative plaques noting important dates in Black history and the civil rights movement. (Credit: Stan Paregien)

From the outset, I knew that the intention of the rehabilitation was to get it approved as a historic landmark in Oklahoma City and, later, in the National Register of Historic Places. The Oklahoma City Historic Preservation Commission deems the three front-facing facades of the building within its realm of consideration. With the three front-facing facades being the brick facades, I decided to add windows to the rear (west) of the building. For the interior, which is not in the commission's purview, I remained faithful to the building in many ways. We left the concrete masonry units exposed and reintroduced the ceiling height changes that were observed in archival photos. Although the painted vinyl flooring will be removed, the concrete floor will be stained with a muted red in one section and blue in another as a nod to the colors selected by Ms. Luper. Similarly, green tiles will be used in the new restrooms to replace the green tiles that had previously been there but were heavily damaged, since the building had been in disrepair for over fifteen years. A small kitchen was added to the building to allow for a variety of community events to occur. I not only wanted to restore the building; I wanted to reestablish the site as a place of

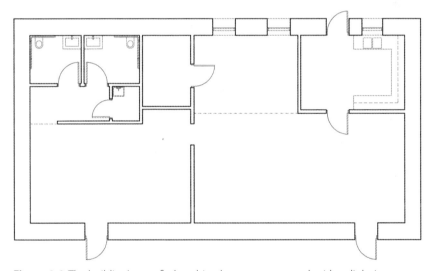

Figure 4-4: The building's post-firebombing layout was restored, with a slight increase to the kitchen size. The Oklahoma City Historic Preservation Commission did not require the interior to be restored. However, given the input from the community, I wanted to allow memories of the space to evoke emotion in the community members who had studied there under Clara Luper and to adhere to our ethos of design, of creating a sense of meaning of place, by having a certain level of devotion to the original building. (Credit: Atelier Cory Henry)

empowerment, and a community resource, as Clara Luper saw it. For me, that also meant (re)envisioning the engagement with the site—the field—itself.

The Field

We did not want the site outside of the building to return to the gas station form or an underutilized patchwork of concrete and asphalt. I proposed that the Freedom Center be considered an artifact, similar to the ones that will be displayed in the future civil rights center, and that we develop the public spaces for the community around it, to maintain and highlight our faithfulness to the building as a symbol of civil rights in Oklahoma City. The Freedom Center building, planned for completion in late 2023, will eventually be part of this three-block cultural corridor, with it and a new civil rights center bookending it. The buildings will weave together the narratives and histories of Oklahoma City's rich civil rights history and future along these three blocks. The building sits on a twenty-thousand-square-foot site on a dimly lit corner. With a limited budget, we created a geometrically designed well-lit field of soft- and hardscaped public spaces for congregating and events. The design creates two lawns for public activities and a hardscaped area, directly in front of the building, as another event space. A series of flora-filled softscape areas and stone seating will demarcate the site as a place of importance. An in-grade LED strip, offset sixty inches from the building, reinforces its importance.

We were aware that there were parties outside of the Northeast Oklahoma City community who wanted to see the building restored to its gas station or white bunker form. When the design was presented to the Oklahoma City Historic Preservation Commission, I advocated for the agency of Clara Luper. I stated that the building should not reflect the conditions of injustice and trauma placed on this community and that the building and site are symbols of the courage of Clara Luper, the many civil rights leaders who fought alongside her, and her students—direct and indirect—who carry on her mission today. That symbol is what we proposed to reestablish through the preservation of the building (frame) and redesign of the site (field). The commission agreed, and the project now has a historic designation.

Figure 4-5: The public space around the Freedom Center was designed to be flexible in order to host events, allow active and passive recreation, and facilitate broad public engagement with the community. (Credit: Atelier Cory Henry)

Construction is underway, and there is a lot of excitement in the community about the project. In an interview for a city news station, Christina Beatty, project director at FCOKC, stated, "It's important for us to tell our story. . . . This is a huge and important part of our history that has not been told." As a Black man in this country, this world, I share the experiences of this community. Nonetheless, I approach each project from a certain outside lens of interest, curiosity, and empathy to understand the perspectives, desires, and emotions in order to tell their story, and enhance their spatial experiences, through design.

Figure 4-6: Trees are added to the site for shade during the summer, making this area a place of reprieve along a boulevard devoid of shade. Stone benches create outdoor spaces at different scales and a space of reflection around the community-designed memorial. (Credit: Atelier Cory Henry)

CHAPTER 5

The Harriet Tubman Memorial, Newark

Nina Cooke John

IN JUNE 2020, IN THE WAKE OF THE MURDER of George Floyd and the protests that followed, we began reckoning with the importance of speaking the full truth of the realities of our past and how they affect our present. Monuments to heroes once revered were being toppled across the globe, and the statue of Christopher Columbus that had stood in Washington Park in Newark, New Jersey, since 1927 was taken down. Mayor Ras Baraka said the removal was "a statement against the barbarism, enslavement, and oppression that this explorer represents." And he acknowledged that it was "in keeping with the movement to remove symbols of oppression and white supremacy."[1] A group of artists and activists danced and played drums as the statue was removed from its pedestal. In the late fall of 2020, the City of Newark announced an artist call for a new monument to Harriet Tubman to be erected at the site previously occupied by the statue of

Columbus. The park was officially renamed Harriet Tubman Square on Juneteenth in 2022.

Finding Embedded Abundance

My work lies along the continuum of art and architecture. I resist a singular definition of Blackness in America by exploring multiplicity in the complex engagement of individuals with urban life and public space. I explore citizenship understood as "the intimate yet complex relation between ourselves and the actual and virtual spaces we inhabit—and the future worlds of which we dream."[2] I aim to create spaces in which we can find belonging, find connection to place, and, as part of the process, encourage a fuller realization of civic engagement. I do this by creating works that relate directly to the scale of the body—spaces that we feel we fit into both when we are by ourselves and when we are with a group. I cannot start any project before getting to know the people and place. The site is understood as layered with deep history that must be uncovered. I must engage with this history of the place, understand the culture of the space and the motivations of the people. I seek to find the abundance already present and where the people find joy in their environment.

Humanizing the Monumental

French writer Édouard Glissant's concept of "opacity" is the resistance to a transparency that, through its all-knowing, reduces the multivariant realities of the Other into an easily digestible flatness. Opacity resists the singular image. It "denies complete incorporation and directs us to ways of being and knowing that are vibrant, untamed, and free-floating . . . opacity strives towards an 'aperture obscurity' such that a type of aesthetic autonomy and resistant Black inhabitation can exist."[3] Opacity, as I understand it, is not opaqueness; it does not exclude but allows the full self to be present. It allows all selves to exist at the same time. All the layered experiences that create the complex realities of our identities as individuals and as a community can claim space.

This is how I approached my understanding of Harriet Tubman throughout the process of designing the monument to her legacy—as a complex individual with layered experiences. The primary intent for the monument was to bring the Newark community into the fold of Harriet Tubman's experience through a personal understanding of liberation within the community space of the monument.

When the artist call for the Harriet Tubman monument first came into my email inbox, I did not respond. I am not a figurative sculptor, which is what I assumed the sponsors of the call wanted for the monument. However, after prompting by a friend, I decided to answer the call. I am the mother of three girls living in nearby Montclair, New Jersey, and I had been following the evolving discourse on monuments and our relationship to them. So I joined the discussion in exploring how the Newark community could engage with a work of art that not only reminds them of the legacy of Harriet Tubman but also allows them to accept her as their own. I would explore how the pride of ownership of the physical place of the monument along with her legacy would create a living monument—a space in which ongoing stories could be made through continued engagement with it.

The recurring questions throughout the process were "What stories belong in public?" and "How do we democratize historical narratives?"

These are critical questions posed by Monument Lab, a nonprofit organization that facilitates ongoing discourse regarding monuments in the United States. Monument Lab defines a monument as "a statement of power and presence in public." The role of monuments in public life—which events should be memorialized, who deserves to be put on pedestals, and who should be remembered—is a contemporary question in both academic and public debates. A key takeaway of the

National Monument Audit led by Monument Lab in 2021 is that "the story of the United States as told by our current monuments misrepresents our history."

> Monuments offer interpretations of the past and play an outsize role in shaping historical narratives and shared memory. In the service of remembering the preferred narratives of their creators, they also can erase, deny, or belittle the historical experience of those who have not had the civic power or privilege to build them. Where inequalities and injustices exist, monuments often perpetuate them.[4]

Top on the list of Monument Lab's vision statements on its website's "About" page is that "monuments must change."

Monument Lab's Re:Generation project asks, "What stories belong in public?" and "How do we democratize historical narratives?" With projects in Rapid City, South Dakota; Los Angeles, California; the Four Corners region, Tucson, Arizona; Puerto Rico; Philadelphia, Pennsylvania; and Queens, New York, the project engages a reimagining of public memory. It investigates the violence against Black women's bodies in Alabama in addressing the pain related to reproductive justice, and the Black femme poets in Philadelphia combine spoken word and sound in the ConsenSIS project. Both projects recenter the voices of women, Black women in particular, whose voices are often muted in public discourse. They also bring the discourse into the present with stories from multiple women, not a single great figure, women who are living and whose stories continue to unfold beyond the project. The power in these projects comes from the combination of multiple voices into one that we cannot silence.

The "great man theory" supports the idea of the solitary hero who is born to power and authority and who is destined to greatness, limiting our capacity to imitate and learn from the hero's deeds. "If our aim is to learn from individuals who somehow rise above their time, we should treat them more like ordinary human beings."[5] The complex story of the civil rights movement is often flattened into a singular, more easily digestible story of Martin Luther King Jr. or Rosa Parks. This erases the multiple hands, hearts, and minds that organized, marched, and died in the service of the long struggle for freedom for all in America. Rosa Parks was one woman. The success of the Montgomery bus boycott took the coordinated efforts of the local branch of the National Association for the Advancement of Colored People (NAACP) along with the maids, cooks, and nannies who walked many miles to and from work to support their right to sit wherever they wanted on a city bus. "Reducing the struggle for civil rights to Martin Luther King and Rosa Parks rightly acknowledges profound personal courage and intelligence, but says little about the thousands of activists whose daily resistance steadily undermined the Jim Crow regime."[6]

The truth of the "great man" that was Christopher Columbus led to the removal of the statue of his likeness in Newark. The removal was met with an uproar by members of the Italian American community in the wider Essex County area. For the Italian American community, the statue was a symbol of Italian American greatness at a time when, as recent immigrants at the beginning of the twentieth century, they were being persecuted. They have voiced their opposition to the project in multiple forums, including in newspaper interviews, at town hall meetings, and at the New Jersey Historic Preservation Office meeting to review the proposed monument to Harriet Tubman. The historic preservation committee denied the application at first, as a result of these protests.

The question of "What stories belong in public space?" is addressed in the installation piece *Will You Be My Monument*. A photograph of a young girl standing in front of the pedestal of the Columbus statue in Harriet Tubman Square soon after it was taken down is mounted on the side of a four-story building a few blocks away. The piece uses reflective acrylic panels to "structurally connect the installation with the pedestal of the original monument and to reflect the diversity and vibrancy of the people of Newark. The sheer size of this installation . . . and its aesthetic gravitas greatly adds to the debates about monuments, racial representation, and social justice, while also enhancing contemporary conversations about the ongoing (in)visibility of Black girls and young women in the United States."[7] The installation, which was a collaboration between writer Salamishah Tillet, designer Chantal Fischzang, and photographer Scheherazade Tillet, claims the space usually taken up by powerful White men for young Black girls, whose voices are historically silenced. Eight-year-old Faa'Tina, pictured in the installation, celebrates her birthday in the park at the time of removal of the statue. Black women can look into her eyes and remember that time on the precipice of adolescence when much seems possible, before hopes are crushed through censure and erasure. It is not the story only of Faa'Tina but the story of Black girlhood.

Newark and Harriet Tubman Square

Newark's history of White flight is very similar to that of cities across the country. There was an influx of African Americans during the great migration; then in the 1950s New Jersey suburbanized, followed by fearmongering realtor practices, redlining, and urban renewal, with the violence and armed conflict of the Newark riots of 1967 encouraging the final wave of flight of Newark's White residents.[8] By 1970, Newark was 54 percent Black, compared with 10 percent in 1940.[9] Newark is still predominantly Black, with a growing Latinx community. Most of the Italian American community has left.

Although Newark is riding a wave of new development, including efforts to revitalize its downtown, Harriet Tubman Square is still underutilized. Military Park, not far from Harriet Tubman Square, underwent major renovations and reopened in 2014. It is now a heavily programmed space with activations and engagement throughout the year. Harriet Tubman Square serves primarily as a walk-through space for students from Rutgers University and employees at Audible's headquarters. Students at the adjacent North Star Academy Charter School sometimes play soccer in the park, and the Newark City Parks Foundation hosts events in the park, but for the most part few people stop to spend any time there.

The Tubman monument sits among several other statues that have long been in the square, including those of George Washington; *Indian and the Puritan* by Gutzon Borglum, the sculptor of Mount Rushmore; and Seth Boyden, the inventor of patent leather and a prominent Newark resident. Considering this, I thought it important that Harriet Tubman should hold her own among the figures of great White men. It was important for me to make her profile in the monument larger than life. She needs to be seen from far away. She needs to be elevated to her rightful place of honor as we give due praise to her achievements: not only as a conductor in the Underground Railroad but also as Union spy, cook, suffragette, and humanitarian for Black causes.

The Harriet Tubman Monument Project

The Harriet Tubman Monument Project, which involves more than the space in the park, is partially funded by the Mellon Foundation's Humanities in Place program. As described by the Mellon Foundation, "Humanities in Place supports a fuller, more complex telling of American histories and lived experiences by deepening the range of how and where our stories are told and by bringing a wider variety of voices into the public dialogue."[10] The larger project brings into the fold existing institutions that are already doing work with the Newark community. In the late fall of 2021, soon after we began developing the design of the monument beyond the initial concept, historians from Rutgers were brought on as consultants to advise and conduct extended historical research on the legacy of the Underground Railroad in Newark. Exhibitions related to Harriet Tubman and the legacy of slavery were commissioned at the Newark Public Library and the Newark Museum of Art (both institutions sit on Harriet Tubman Square), and the museum is working with the Newark Public School District to integrate the historical research and accompanying exhibitions into the public school curriculum and tours. The museum has coordinated Community Day events to engage patrons of all ages with the legacy of Harriet Tubman and the Black Liberation struggle in Newark. The overall vision has been solidly grounded in the office of the mayor of Newark.

Harriet Tubman

In my concept submission video, I invited everyone to imagine the Harriet Tubman within themselves, all of them struggling toward liberation of one kind or another.

> I am Harriet Tubman . . .
> You are Harriet Tubman . . .
> We are all Harriet Tubman pushing, climbing, crawling to some
>   other shore.
> I am Harriet Tubman
> You are Harriet Tubman
> We are all Harriet Tubman looking back, pulling up, carrying our
>   kindred as far as they need to go.
> I am Harriet Tubman
> You are Harriet Tubman

> We are all Harriet Tubman looking for a place to rest, to lay down
>   our load and to be FREE.
> We are all Harriet Tubman looking for the comfort of friends and
>   family when we get to the other side.[11]

I knew that Harriet Tubman was many things—scout, spy, cook, suffragette, and, famously, conductor on the Underground Railroad. She was stronger than many men, led many people out of slavery, and cared for and protected those in need. She did things that most of us could not imagine having the strength to do. We must honor her. We must put her on a pedestal. We must claim the space she justly deserves.

There is more to Harriet Tubman than we think we know. We can never know her fully, nor should we ever elevate our heroes such that they are not understood as being human. It is in their humanity that we see ourselves. She was a trusted sister, a faithful friend and daughter. As we get to know her as a woman, we can connect with her. We see ourselves in her. She can help to show us the way. Help us to liberate ourselves from the woes that plague us today. Harriet Tubman did not act alone; her story is about community. Harriet Tubman's profound sense of loneliness upon crossing over the line into freedom without her family speaks to the universal need for connection.

> I had crossed the line. I was free; but there was no one to welcome
>   me to the land of freedom. I was a stranger in a strange land; and
>   my home, after all, was down in Maryland; because my father, my
>   mother, my brothers, and sisters, and friends were there. But I was
>   free, and they should be free.[12]

Harriet Tubman was "driven by her desire to liberate her family and friends, guided by an unquestioning belief in God's protection, and confident in the vast underground network she had come to know so well."[13] These secret networks were built in the antebellum equivalents to public space: markets, horse races, and camp meetings. The enslaved journeyed miles to hear the messages of hope among biblical text that were different from those of obedience that they heard at the churches of their masters. They walked for hours not only to hear the gospel of liberation today (not a promised liberation in the afterlife) but also to meet with and build connections with the enslaved from other estates. These connections were the foundation for the secret codes that would give the Underground Railroad the capacity to liberate as many as one hundred thousand people. An intricate network of codes indicated safe houses, signaled safe arrivals, or signified that it was safe to dock at otherwise treacherous harbors.

The Power of Networks and Importance of Public Space

The strength of the network of the Underground Railroad was extremely important during the era of slavery, and community networks are still extremely important today. We build these networks in public space. We build community in places in which we can live our lives in the open. When we march together through the streets, we are strengthened by the bodies moving ahead of us and those behind us. We feel our voices mixing with others to create a union that is stronger than the individual. When we sit on park benches, we enjoy our solitude in spite of, or because of, the hustle and bustle of the urban environment around us. We feel connected to others enjoying the space, whether we share words with them or not. The Harriet Tubman monument was designed to act as a meeting place, a place of connection for the people of Newark via the legacy of the Underground Railroad and the contributions of past citizens of Newark.

Monument Design—*Shadow of a Face*

Hoot-owl calling in the ghosted air,
five times calling to the hants in the air.
Shadow of a face in the scary leaves,
shadow of a voice in the talking leaves.[14]
　　—"Runagate Runagate" by Robert Hayden

From the open call, five artists were short-listed, and I was one of them. I was the only architect. All artists had to submit their concept along with a description of community engagement to accompany the design. I dedicated the design of the monument to the women of Newark. The women who save lives every day. The women who travel into the wilderness to seek salvation. The women who create and sustain the networks that help lead us all into salvation—women who come with swords up. We all know who they are, though they don't always recognize themselves. The monument aims to help them recognize themselves in the woman that Harriet Tubman was. We understand that being Harriet is hard. Some of us have to be the pulling Harriet; some of us have to be the pushing Harriet. Some of us don't yet realize that we are Harriet. So, though we lift her up in the monument, we also connect with her as her face appears on one of the walls at eye level. We see our face in hers.

At the center of the monument, which I named *Shadow of a Face* from a line of the poem "Runagate, Runagate" portraying the Underground Railroad by Robert Hayden, the first African American poet laureate, is the twenty-five-foot-high abstracted central figure of Harriet Tubman. Her face emerges from a lower wall, the Portrait Wall. These are the two key representative elements of *Shadow of a Face*—addressing the duality of the monumental and the everyday. I explored this duality,

Figure 5-1: Plan view of the monument as submitted for the competition. (Image: Studio Cooke John)

asking, "How do I, as a public artist, elevate Harriet Tubman within the park among the other monuments while allowing people to connect to her? How do I convey the multifaceted nature of this icon?" As an artist, I start by making with my hands. That intuitive connection between my processing of ideas in my head with their physical articulation is studied through collage and multiple iterations of study models.

I start the design with the circle. The circle provides the groundwork out of which all the forms grow. At the center is the abstracted figure of Harriet Tubman—her profile extruded in steel and rotated three times around its central axis. The circle ripples out and multiplies, then shifts and opens up. The resulting overlapping geometry of circles creates the base of the Learning Wall and the Portrait Wall. The shifted circles create interlocking paths that allow a meditative, labyrinthine movement in, through, and around the different elements of the monument. The

Figure 5-2: View at night. (Photo: Tracy Collins, Three Cee Media)

circles also reference the cosmograms of African and African American tradition, which connect people across space and time. As the circle grounds the monument, it connects us to one another, connects us to our ancestors, and connects us to our children yet to be born. The circle is broken by the footprint of Columbus's statue—a ghosted memory that it had stood there.

Along the outer surface of the Learning Wall, where a timeline of Tubman's life is etched in the wood surface, we learn key details of her life, opening up our understanding of her full life experience beyond the little that we know, legible for those seeing and blind. We walk under a steel trellis and sinews extending from the central figure and over the Learning Wall mimicking her protective cloak while signifying the network that guided her. Along the inner surface of the Learning Wall, etched in the Corten steel panels, are the liberation stories of the

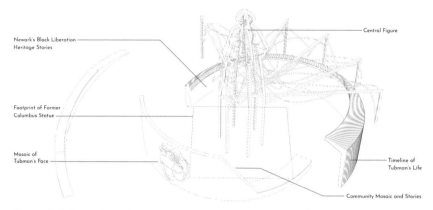

Newark's Black Liberation
Heritage Stories

Footprint of Former
Columbus Statue

Mosaic of
Tubman's Face

Central Figure

Timeline of
Tubman's Life

Community Mosaic and Stories

Figure 5-3: Illustration of monument components as seen on the interpretive signage in the park. (Image: Studio Cooke John)

multiple groups based in Newark who contributed to the efforts of the Underground Railroad.

The path connects to the Portrait Wall, where Harriet Tubman's face emerges in relief made up of a mosaic of large concrete pieces. The pieces create a texture that encourages touch. The texture of the mosaic is repeated, at a different scale, on the inner surface of the Portrait Wall using ceramic pieces, each with the story of a different Newark resident collected at workshops conducted throughout the city. The mosaics reinforce that this is a monument for the community by the community and that Harriet's story is their story. It also adds to the multisensory experience of the monument. We look up from our touch of the mosaic to understand the complex greatness that is Harriet Tubman as her figure rises above us, the profile lit at night, acting as a beacon to those who are seeking her. Guiding the way. The height of the Portrait Wall reduces from ten feet at the face to seventeen inches at a bench encouraging sitting, staying, and contemplation. A second bench emerges from the outermost arc at the edge of the green space of the park. From this perch, visitors can engage with the monument in one direction or with the larger park in the other—a more casual engagement as people walk through or sit in the park or coordinate protests as part of their civic engagement. The space is designed to accommodate and provide a backdrop to performances of many kinds: poetry readings, dance performances, and martial arts exhibitions.

Figure 5-4: View of monument looking toward wood-clad Learning Wall and mosaic wall beyond. (Photo: Nina Cooke John)

Speakers are embedded in the Learning Wall and Portrait Wall. An algorithm controls a mix of twenty-second clips of narration of Harriet Tubman's life, of the stories of Newark's Black Liberation groups, and of stories collected during the community workshops. This monument is a living memorial to the everyday lives of all the Harriets of Newark. The stories of the past are combined with the stories of the present in this immersive experience.

The Design Process

As part of the design proposal submitted in March 2021, I stressed that it was important that the people of Newark would be able to tell their own stories of personal liberation. Over the course of a year, after *Shadow of a Face* was announced as the winning design in June 2021, we held workshops at the Newark Museum of Art and the Newark Public Library—both on Harriet Tubman Square close to the site of the new monument, as well as at Express Newark (a Rutgers affiliate), Harriet R. Tubman Elementary School, local galleries, and community safe houses. The workshops were a core component of the community engagement and the compilation of the mosaics described in the concept proposal. Adebunmi Gbadebo, a Newark-based artist, worked as my community-based apprentice, helping to identify locations for the engagement sessions and coordinating the outreach. During the workshops, we introduced participants to the design concepts of the monument and invited them to share their own stories. All the designs from the five short-listed artists had been posted on a public website with public comments; however, many, many people still had no idea that the monument was being designed or what it would look like. I designed a process that included worksheets with prompts from which community members, young and old, responded to the primary questions of "Who was Harriet Tubman?" and "What does liberation mean to you?" They etched the symbols of their stories into clay tiles, which were fired and glazed and will become part of a mosaic on the wall of the monument. It was important to me that they had a physical engagement with the clay while creating artifacts that became part of the monument. The workshops also provided an opportunity for community members to share their stories orally. We created quiet rooms at the workshops in which they could choose either to be interviewed or to respond privately to prompts. We set up a recording booth at the Newark Public Library where residents could come in on their own time to record themselves. These responses form a vocal mosaic of the spectrum of people's connection to what they understand Harriet Tubman's legacy to be and of their varied stories of liberation.

Shadow of a Face will be a place of pilgrimage. People will visit the monument from all corners of Newark and New Jersey. They will come to learn about Harriet Tubman and to connect with her. In the process, they will connect with themselves and get one step closer to their own liberation from whatever weight they might be carrying. When they come, they will find a place that is welcoming, that encourages them to sit and stay. Their experiences will be multisensory, providing opportunities for engagement through sound and touch in addition to sight.

The Stories Continue On

The monument was unveiled in March 2023, coinciding with the anniversary of Harriet Tubman's birthday, March 10. The Newark Museum of Art engaged residents, young and old, in a Community Day celebration with theatrical performances, music, poetry, and tours of the monument.

On follow-up visits to the site, I witnessed people searching for, finding, and taking photos next to their tiles, now embedded in the mosaic of the monument. I spoke to a pair of retired teachers from the Newark school system who had made the trip from neighboring towns to visit. I saw a young girl sitting on the outer bench doing homework while her mother walked through with a friend. On a Saturday afternoon, a group of four children ran in and around the curved walls and jumped on and off the benches, and the youngest girl kissed Harriet Tubman's lips. When public art goes out into the world, it becomes a part of the community and belongs to the people who engage with it. The Newark

Museum of Art, the Newark Public Library, Audible, and the Newark City Parks Foundation are all committed to continued programming and activation of the park to ensure that it comes to life as a space of continued community storytelling.

CHAPTER 6

Materializing Memory: The Camp Barker Memorial in Washington, DC

Katie MacDonald and Kyle Schumann

THE CAMP BARKER MEMORIAL, DESIGNED IN 2017 and constructed in 2019 on the historic site of a Civil War–era "contraband camp," demonstrates an empathic approach to surfacing and constructing memory in public space. The project shows how nontraditional architectural practice through the commissioning of a public artwork can become a vehicle for engaging emotion and memory in the design process.

Two types of historical markers commonly register the legacy of the American Civil War in the built environment: monuments and memorials. Art critic Arthur C. Danto addressed their differences in his review of the Vietnam Veterans Memorial:

> We erect monuments so that we shall always remember, and build memorials so that we shall never forget. . . . Monuments commemorate the memorable and embody the myths of beginnings.

Memorials ritualize remembrance and mark the reality of ends. . . .
Monuments make heroes and triumphs, victories and conquests,
perpetually present and part of life. The memorial is a special pre-
cinct, extruded from life, a segregated enclave where we honor the
dead. With monuments, we honor ourselves.[1]

Danto's definition explicitly links monuments with conceptions of
self. People immortalize their present interpretations of the past through
the design and placement of monuments. In turn, these markers become
a vehicle to define and gain access to history—to frame what should
be remembered in relationship to present values. It follows that monuments are often politicized, given that they attempt to mythologize,
heroize, and shape prevailing narratives of self.

In the same vein, many Confederate monuments were built not to
remember the dead but in an attempt to recapture and redefine the
identity of the American South decades after the end of the Civil War.
There were two distinct spikes in the construction and dedication of
Confederate monuments in the United States: first, when Southern
states were enacting Jim Crow laws: 349 monuments between 1900 and
the outbreak of World War I in 1914; and second, during the modern
civil rights movement: 91 monuments from 1954 to 1968.[2]

Figure 6-1: Plan of Monument Avenue in Richmond, Virginia, circa 1933. (Image com-
piled by authors from drawings by the Historic American Buildings Survey. "Monument
Avenue, Richmond [Independent City], VA." Photograph retrieved from the Library of
Congress, www.loc.gov/item/va1670/)

In Richmond, Virginia, Monument Avenue was designed not only as a series of Confederate monuments but also as a grand urban gesture, in the tradition of the City Beautiful movement (figure 6-1). Explicit in the monumental grandeur of the boulevard was the promotion of the Lost Cause, a pseudohistorical, negationist mythology that decoupled the abolition of slavery from the causes of the Civil War. Between 1890 and 1929, five Confederate monuments were installed within the forty-foot-wide tree-lined median along the five-mile-long, 130-foot-wide avenue. Each statue was crafted in the tradition of heroic monumentality, elevated above the viewer on a plinth. Monument Avenue's namesake monuments varied in size from the modestly scaled seated Matthew Fontaine Maury to the equestrian Robert E. Lee statue, towering sixty feet above the street, and the Jefferson Davis memorial, featuring a sixty-seven-foot-tall Doric column and large semicircular colonnade.

Farther south, Stone Mountain, located near Atlanta, Georgia, was the site of Ku Klux Klan activity beginning in 1915. Efforts were made to plan a Confederate monument on the site, and in 1958, the state purchased the land in order to realize these plans.[3] The entrenched site was invoked by Martin Luther King Jr. in his iconic 1963 speech on the National Mall: "Let freedom ring from Stone Mountain of Georgia."[4] The state-owned stone was inscribed from 1964 to 1972 with a three-acre bas-relief depicting three Confederate heroes—an apparent rebuke of the civil rights movement (1954–1968).[5] Today, the immense

sculpture is referred to as a memorial, but its roots stem from the planning efforts of the Stone Mountain Monumental Association, affirming that the project is more accurately described as a monument meant to mythologize the Confederacy. The association claims the monument to be "the largest relief sculpture in the world," with figures measuring 90 by 190 feet, carved to a depth of 42 feet, with a total carved area of three acres (figure 6.2).[6] Groups such as the Stone Mountain Action Coalition are actively seeking the removal of Confederate symbols and names from Stone Mountain. An ongoing legal debate centers on what constitutes an "appropriate and suitable memorial for the Confederacy."[7] In 2021, Confederate flags were relocated, but not removed from, the state-owned park.[8]

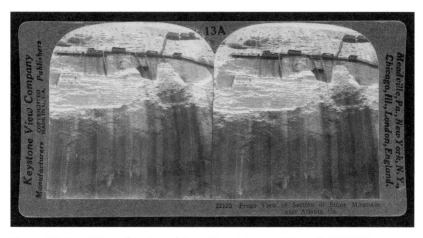

Figure 6-2: "Front View of Section of Stone Mountain near Atlanta, Ga," 1928. (Retrieved from the Library of Congress, www.loc.gov/item/2018647300/)

Applied to Civil War historical markers, Danto's dichotomy between monument and memorial might be understood in this way: Confederate monuments create memories—they mythologize—whereas memorials remember. Understood through this lens, the Camp Barker Memorial is conceived as an act of remembrance. It marks the location of a Civil

War–era contraband camp, Camp Barker, on the site of the modern-day Garrison Elementary School, a public school in Washington, DC.

The design and realization of the Camp Barker Memorial by our practice, After Architecture, aligns with rising regional, national, and international discourse on the role of Civil War markers in the built environment and a reckoning with their emotional impacts on marginalized communities and the broader public. In 2015, the murder of nine worshippers at the Emanuel African Methodist Episcopal Church in Charleston, South Carolina, spurred national discussion over the persistence of Confederate imagery in the public realm. In August 2017, the Unite the Right rally in Charlottesville, Virginia, was a hostile response to plans to remove a Confederate monument of Robert E. Lee, further inflaming discourse at the national level. In 2020, the murder of George Floyd prompted international protests. Confederate monuments, as prominent public symbols of oppression, were often chosen as locations for public demonstration and became central to an expanding conversation about monuments across the globe. Notably, Monument Avenue's particularly grand urban gesture and edification of Confederate heroes reached a tipping point, and its Confederate heroes were removed by 2021.

A counterpoint to the Confederate monument, the Camp Barker Memorial was first designed in May 2017, months before the rally in Charlottesville, and installed in May 2019, a year before George Floyd's murder. Against this backdrop, the Camp Barker Memorial marks a piece of Civil War history specific to the experience of those leaving captivity and provides an alternative approach to traditional historical markers. The project is intentionally framed as a memorial, not a monument. Its aim is not to politicize nor mythologize but to reveal an unseen history. In line with Danto's definition of a memorial, the project honors the dead, but its primary function is to physically mark the site and manifest memory on a public stage, a reminder of the past brought into the present.

Freedmen and Contraband Camps

The contraband camp typology came into existence shortly after the outbreak of the American Civil War, as an immediate result of the Confiscation Act of 1861. The act of Congress classified enslaved persons as "contrabands of war," granting quasi-freedom to those who reached Union territories, who were legally considered to be captured enemy property. Also known as freedmen villages, contraband camps were meagerly outfitted and overcrowded residential communities erected by the government for the newly liberated. Over the course of the war, four to five hundred thousand women, children, and men lived in such camps.[9] The design of such spaces was not deliberate and studied but a rushed product of circumstance. Existing structures were repurposed by the government with little investment, becoming refuges to thousands of human beings whose personhood and individual rights were only just starting to be legally recognized in the United States.

Camp Barker (1862–1863), a contraband camp located in the northeastern quadrant of Washington, DC, near Logan Circle, was built as a collection of army barracks for Union soldiers. The camp consisted of a series of two-story linear timber-frame buildings, raised slightly above the swampy terrain and connected by wooden boardwalks.[10] This utilitarian layout, while sufficient for a small population of male soldiers preparing for war, lacked the spatial and social planning necessary to provide adequate communal infrastructure and residential quarters for the large number of formerly enslaved people who took shelter there. One account described the camp in simple metrics: "Near the corner of Twelfth and Q streets, on the same ground formerly occupied by Coltman's brick kilns and St. John's burial ground, and at present [November 1862] contains 675 persons, among whom are about 100 in the hospital; the balance being women and children."[11]

Some eleven thousand people would dwell at Camp Barker over its

Figure 6-3: "Freedman's Village," 1862–1865. "The White House Historical Association describes this photo as depicting the residents of Camp Barker as they prepared for Lincoln's visit." (Freedman's Village, Arlington [i.e., Alexandria], Virginia. Photographed between 1862 and 1865, printed between 1880 and 1889. Retrieved from the Library of Congress, www.loc.gov/item/2014645761/)

seventeen-month run, as many as four thousand at a time, but planning failures resulted in the camp's short tenure.[12] By the end of 1863, inadequate sanitation infrastructure resulted in an outbreak of disease and closure of the camp. Despite its short operation, the camp had a lasting impact on its immediate surrounds. While some occupants relocated to Freedman's Village at Arlington Cemetery, others purchased property nearby, leading to the formation of a long-standing community in the heart of the capital.[13]

Camp Barker's temporal nature resulted in little documentation of its facilities or the lives of its occupants. President Abraham Lincoln came to know Camp Barker because of its location near the capital—it was located along the route he rode from the White House to his summer residence, the Soldiers' Home, known today as President Lincoln's Cottage (figure 6.3).[14]

Commissioning Memory

Garrison Elementary School stands where Camp Barker once was, occupying three sides of an urban block at the corner of S Street NW and Vermont Avenue NW. This neighborhood is home to the Logan Circle African American Heritage Trail, a network of historic sites celebrating writers, artists, and civil rights leaders who called the neighborhood home. The neighborhood's proximity to Howard University, just to the northeast, made it a vibrant intellectual community during the Black Renaissance in Washington, DC, in the 1920s.

The Garrison Elementary School grounds were renovated in 2019 and now contain an artificial turf soccer and baseball field, a basketball court, and several playgrounds for children of various ages. It is one of the largest parks in the area and a popular destination for both adult and youth recreation activities outside of school hours and on weekends. Until recently, there was no visible trace of the site's history except for a small informational sign across an adjacent intersection.

The Camp Barker Memorial was commissioned through a process atypical of the planning of monuments and memorials. The project was not proposed as an entry to a design competition or a coordinated public effort to uncover the site's history but through the Percent for Art program operated by the Washington, DC, Department of General Services as part of the elementary school's 2017–2019 renovation. Many cities across the country run such programs to integrate art and design into public spaces and streetscapes. DC's Percent for Art program began in 2013 and requires that 1 percent of the construction budget of large-scale public building projects in the district be used to commission public artwork.[15] The program operates through a multi-stage commissioning process, first collecting sample works from applicants and then inviting several of them to develop and present design proposals to a professional and community jury.

At the beginning of the 2017 renovation, the school's Percent for Art budget was organized to be split between five pieces, each by a different artist, including a playground sculpture, a lobby wall installation, and a series of entry markers framed as three separate commissions. The initial public call or request for qualifications (RFQ) made mention of Camp Barker as a notable moment in a description of the site's history but contained no specific requirements as to whether or how this history should be engaged in design proposals. In this RFQ phase, we were selected as finalists for one of the entry markers. In the request for proposals (RFP) stage, nine artist and designer teams presented specific design proposals for the three entry marker sites to a jury of school staff, renovation architects, Department of General Services team members, and community representatives.

Early in the design process, we considered how our intervention could hold meaning beyond marking an entry to the school grounds. The history of Camp Barker quickly captivated our attention as a historic moment that was not visible on the contemporary site but shaped the present-day community. Marking Camp Barker presented an opportunity to make tangible an influential period in the collective memory of the neighborhood, around which the community could come together. We began an iterative design process exploring many possible schemes that shared the memory of Camp Barker with an audience of both schoolchildren and the general public. In the design presentation, we conveyed the history of Camp Barker, why it should be memorialized, and how this could be done in a sensitive way. Our design proposed that the three separate commissions at the site boundary could be combined into a single cohesive scheme of three entry portals, together marking the site's history as a contraband camp.

The community representatives on the jury responded to our design's focus on Camp Barker and the idea that in order to properly mark the site, all three entry locations needed to be designed together. Feedback was provided on drawings, images, and a physical model representing the intended material palette. In particular, the committee identified the need to convey a literal or figural representation of the site's historical narrative, to broaden access to the memory of Camp Barker. Our portal design was selected to be adapted to each of the three site boundary locations and combined with a proposal by sculptor Vinnie Bagwell, who had designed a series of blackened bronze reliefs tying the site's history to significant milestones in African American history. This collaboration ultimately allowed two distinct proposals aimed at memorializing Camp Barker to become one stronger and cohesive series of interventions, while the other three artworks selected for the campus took form as discrete interventions engaging themes of play and wonder.

Tight budgets, complex project requirements, and limited control over construction sometimes preclude opportunities to meaningfully engage history in traditional project delivery by architects. The commissioning of the Camp Barker Memorial provides an example of how nontraditional forms of practice and additional services can be leveraged by architects to take on new agency in defining what is unearthed and framed in the built environment. Public art calls are often framed around a particular type of siting—for example, hanging lobby art, outdoor sculpture, facade installation, or public seating—but usually do not include any specific instructions for the program or function, creating programming opportunities for the artist. Additionally, because artists deliver the physical artifact, acting more akin to a design-build delivery model of practice, greater control over the physical execution of the design is possible.

Materializing Memory

In defining the plan of Washington, DC, Pierre Charles L'Enfant choreographed grandiose intersections of avenues to stage a heroic vision of democratic life. This axiality, punctuated by gleaming white masonry monuments, professed democracy and shared governance for some, notably excluding enslaved people, women, and those without the wealth to purchase land. Its ideals were rooted in a monumental architecture and defensive urban planning characteristic of powerful governments and their leaders, and classical elements drew from the birthplace of Western civilization, Greece. In effect, this architectural language is tied to a select population and does not celebrate the histories or values of the broader public.

The Camp Barker Memorial distinguishes itself from both the urban approach of the capital and the materiality of its buildings and monuments. In contrast to the tradition of objectified and heroic figural monuments on pedestals, each memorial portal sits at ground level. Unlike many figural monuments in the capital, which sit as objects at the center of urban spaces, the portals are incorporated into the school ground's perimeter fence and streetscape design (figure 6.4). The portals form a threshold to pass through when entering or leaving the site. Their tapered geometries in plan extend to the surrounding sidewalk, which widens as it reaches the street, welcoming passersby to enter the school ground and park (figure 6.5). Operable gates can be closed during school day play and disappear flush into the portal surface when open.

The largest of the three entry gateways, a triple portal, faces the arterial street of Vermont Avenue, a diagonal boulevard that connects Logan Circle, Thomas Circle, McPherson Square, and Lafayette Square, which lies in front of the White House. Located adjacent to the basketball court and playground, the three linked portals alternate between convex and concave orientations, inviting engagement from both sides (figure 6.6). The large central threshold is flanked by two smaller ones, which can be entered and occupied from the playground side, inviting children to inhabit the memorial (figure 6.7).

The modesty of construction that characterizes the original barracks buildings that constituted Camp Barker informs the design of

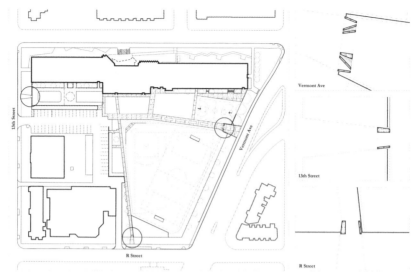

Figure 6-4: Plan showing portal locations along the perimeter of the school grounds. (Drawing by After Architecture)

Figure 6-5: View northeast on approach to the 13th Street NW portal. (Photo by Sam Oberter)

Figure 6-6: View southwest on approach to the Vermont Avenue NW portal. (Photo by Sam Oberter)

Figure 6-7: View east from the playground to the Vermont Avenue NW portal. (Photo by Sam Oberter)

the memorial and differentiates it from the surrounding contemporary streetscape. Like the long-gone barracks that once existed on the site, the memorial is built with a simple timber-frame structure. Timber cladding is transformed, borrowing the Japanese *shou sugi ban* technique, from modest to precious. The rich, dark hue contrasts with the gleaming marble masonry, putting forth an alternative material ethos. The wood is subjected to extremes through burning the exterior, which forms a layer of char that is both functional and aesthetic: it gains resilience to solar ultraviolet rays, water, and insects while taking on an intensely beautiful texture, depth, and color.

The abstract geometry of the portals is complemented by narrative sculptural reliefs incorporated into the street-facing surface of each threshold. Authored by sculptor Vinnie Bagwell, the reliefs are cast in blackened bronze and set into the charred wood facade (figure 6.8). A major adaptation to the portal's original design included thickening each portal on one side, creating a place to install and display the vertical sculptural panels. It was important that the narratives conveyed in the reliefs faced the street, presenting themselves as primary ways of understanding, connecting with, and experiencing the memorial.

Contrasting with the charred wood exterior, the interior surfaces are clad in sheets of naval brass. The brass is reflective but not highly polished, producing blurred reflections that transform the individuality of each visitor into a generic human silhouette. Reflected light casts a golden hue across the surrounding site. The brass takes on the wear of daily life as a patina and record of time. While a sense of importance is often conveyed in monuments through massive masonry or marble elements, a sense of reverence is conveyed through the warmth and color of the thin brass liner. The brass is not a painting or a coating but a substantial layer of material, such that it can form a patina over time as the public touches and interacts with it.

We worked with a team of collaborators and consultants to realize the portals. This included a structural engineer and fabricator to specify, approve, and build the portal's structural frames, and teams to transport and install the portals and relief sculptures on-site. We completed much of the finishing work on the portals, including charring and installing the oak exterior as well as detailing and installing the brass interior.

While working on-site during the memorial's construction, we spoke with many passersby (figure 6.9). Many were excited for design work that could surface a cultural memory. Others questioned the black hue of the memorial, asking what color we planned to paint the structures. Some wondered whether the portals, placed around a school, were metal detectors—they are not—bringing another contemporary American challenge into the conversation. Journalist Sharine Taylor's independent review of the project describes the Camp Barker Memorial as "a hauntingly jarring but necessary cultural project" that "compels us to question who—and what—needs protecting."[16]

Empathic Memory

Camp Barker marks one intervention in an expanding body of projects by contemporary architects, artists, and designers that interrogate American history, uncovering stories unacknowledged by the prevailing cultural narratives of past eras. Public scholar Renée Ater's "Contemporary Monuments to the Slave Past" catalogs such works in an evolving online database of monuments and memorials relating to the global trade of enslaved people, while in this volume, Elgin Cleckley defines an empathic approach to design that underlies many such projects.[17] The fact that such work is being made—and inventoried—across the United States marks a shift in the cultural narratives being foregrounded and the role architects play in bringing forward these histories. The agency of architects and designers in such projects, particularly in those commissioned as public artworks, introduces alternative modes of practice

Figure 6-8: Detail of bronze relief on the 13th Street NW portal. View southeast. (Photo by After Architecture)

Figure 6-9: View northeast across the school grounds to the Vermont Avenue NW portal. (Photo by Sam Oberter)

in which architecture is not solely in service of a client's desires but has the capacity to enter into a dialogue with communities and surface public memory. Across such projects, the language of memory is expanding: the Classical motifs and heroic monumentality commonly found in government buildings, public spaces, and urban design in the United States must be reconsidered in light of the narrow lineage they invoke, and new materials and forms can build out a more nuanced, varied terrain. Rather than work to mythologize, architects today would do well to remember.

CHAPTER 7

Practicing _mpathic design: The Charlottesville Memorial for Peace and Justice

Elgin Cleckley

"How can I have more empathy in my design work?" is a question I am often asked by designers. It has been asked more frequently since the murder of George Floyd in 2020 as design organizations and designers have made personal and public calls for action to dismantle our long history of spatial injustice in design-related fields. This question is a catalyst for this book. My public scholarship aims to shift empathy away from being thought of as a quick step for capital gain, as in popular design-thinking processes.

I've spent over two and a half decades formulating a spatial understanding of empathy in academic, community, and professional design contexts that I call _mpathic design. The missing "e" in "_mpathy" and "_mpathic" is purposeful. Its absence symbolizes the act of removing any exaggerated sense of self or ego in the design process. Being _mpathic asks designers to create meetings, workshops, and interactions fostering co-creative relationships of trust—making space for emotions to be shared with affected communities to shape the design. It's also about doing the internal work as designers to expand our imagination and creativity for meaningful, equitable, and inclusive design futures.

_mpathic design is the title of my initiatives, pedagogy (I also teach at the University of Virginia's School of Architecture), and professional practice. At its core is a process I developed, creating designs in public spaces that translate, acknowledge, reflect, and connect with untold, marginalized narratives. My approach recognizes the emotions marginalized identities feel from the designs in public spaces.

In *Empathy: A History*, Susan Lanzoni explains that the origins of "empathy" are in the German term *Einfühlung* ("in-feeling"), from Robert Vischer and Theodor Lipps in 1908.[1] "In-feeling" is an aesthetic activity of transferring one's own feelings into the forms and shapes of objects.[2] Lanzoni explains that these feelings are "extensions of the self—imagined, projected, or extended—into others and the world" and that these "connections [are] bound by feeling, and often incorporating knowing and bodily awareness."[3] Being a Black man, I'm constantly aware of what it's like to move through public spaces. I'm continually adjusting, feeling, or reacting to the true meanings of their designs, especially in Charlottesville, Virginia, where I live. "In-feeling" is heightened in public space by the *layers*—social, cultural, historical, economic, political, environmental, and natural—seen and unseen. My process helps designers discover the layers related to untold, marginalized narratives—achieving what Lonnie Bunch, educator, historian, and fourteenth secretary of the Smithsonian Institution, tells us, that untold spatial histories are "hiding in plain sight."[4]

Being _mpathic shifts "in-feeling" to "feeling with"—so that marginalized identities feel comfortable in a public space's co-created designs. The goal is for marginalized communities to say, "I see myself here now," "I feel connected," "I feel represented by this," and "My story is told here." I'll demonstrate my process in a case study from my practice, the Charlottesville Memorial for Peace and Justice (CMPJ). The CMPJ, dedicated on July 12, 2019, is a memorial to John Henry James in Charlottesville's Court Square. As described in the introduction to this book, James was a Black ice-cream salesman falsely accused of assaulting Julia Hotopp, a White woman from an esteemed Charlottesville family, on July 11, 1898. John Henry James was lynched just west of town at Wood's Crossing on July 12, 1898, by an unmasked White mob.

Case Study: Charlottesville Memorial for Peace and Justice

In the spring of 2019, Siri Russell, then director of the Albemarle County Office of Equity and Diversity (ACOED), asked my practice to provide a design for the Charlottesville Memorial for Peace and Justice in our city's Court Square. Siri explained that the CMPJ would consist of a historical marker from the Equal Justice Initiative's (EJI's) Community Historical Marker Project and one of the eight hundred duplicate six-foot Corten steel body column monuments created by EJI and MASS Design Group from the National Memorial for Peace and Justice in Montgomery, Alabama.

Memorials for Peace and Justice, such as Charlottesville's, are planned for each county in the United States where lynchings occurred—over 4,400 documented by EJI. EJI tells untold narratives of racial terror in public space through two empathic initiatives within the Community Remembrance Project, which "partners with community coalitions to memorialize documented victims of racial violence throughout history and foster meaningful dialogue about race and justice today."[5]

First, the Community Soil Collection Project collects soil at lynching sites in glass jars for display in the Legacy Museum in Montgomery. Second, the Historical Marker Project places descriptive markers where the violence occurred.[6] In July 2018, a collaboration of local government agencies, community organizers, leaders, residents, and members from the University of Virginia participated in the Community Remembrance Project, marking the lynching of John Henry James by collecting a jar of soil in a public ceremony at Wood's Crossing, followed by a pilgrimage to deliver the jar for inclusion in a permanent exhibition at the Legacy Museum.[7] Soon after, plans began for installing the historical marker and the six-foot body column in Charlottesville's Court Square.

The Untold Narrative

Charlottesville writer Brendan Wolfe describes the untold narrative of John Henry James in "The Train at Wood's Crossing," taking us back to the morning of July 11, 1898:

> As Hotopp approached the farm on her newly shod horse, she noticed something out of place. Rather than fastened with a latch, the gate was bound with wire. Why? What was the point of that? She turned in her saddle and looked around for farm hands, for anyone, but the area was deserted.
>
> After dismounting, she unwound the wire and freed the gate.
>
> "As she turned to remount," the *Daily Progress* newspaper reported in that afternoon's edition, "someone approached her from behind and struck her, and then grasped her by the neck, forcing her to the ground, when she became unconscious."
>
> When she came to, it was about ten o'clock. Her assailant had disappeared and so had her horse. A few minutes later, though, she spied her brother Carl running in her direction, the riderless mount having tipped him off. She scrambled to her feet and walked gingerly in his direction.
>
> "Upon meeting her brother," the paper wrote, "she swooned again."

Back at the house and off her feet, Julia Hotopp was finally able to describe what had happened to her. Her assailant, she said, had been "a very black man, heavy-set, slight mustache," who had worn dark clothes. His toes, she recalled, had stuck out of his shoes.[8]

Earlier that day, James was apprehended by authorities in Dudley's bar on East Main Street. It was reported in the local newspaper, the *Charlottesville Daily Progress*, that James "answer[ed] somewhat the description of Miss Hotopp's assailant." Instead of being held at the county jail at Court Square, James was taken by officials west to Staunton to avoid the lynch mobs gathering at the jail. When officials returned James the next day by train, a mob of White men intercepted his train just west of town at Wood's Crossing, about six miles from Court Square. After overpowering a group of Black citizens who stood in their way, they attached a noose to James's neck, strung him up in a tree, and shot him multiple times. Hotopp's brother emptied his revolver into James. Parts of his clothing and body were kept as souvenirs.[9] John Henry James was posthumously indicted at the courthouse in Court Square.

Community Context

Charlottesville's community of care has long been dedicated to creating inclusive and equitable public spaces. Participating in the Community Remembrance Project meant that the untold narrative was well known by the spring of 2019, with the pilgrimage well publicized in local media. The Jefferson School African American Heritage Center also displayed a jar of the collected soil from the lynching site in a free public exhibition created by the center's director, Dr. Andrea Douglas, telling James's story.

University of Virginia student activist Zyahna Bryant's petition to remove the Robert E. Lee statue in Charlottesville and rename the park led to a wave of community support, guiding the Charlottesville City Council's public hearings and votes to remove the Confederate statues. Our community had known for years of the true history of the Confederate statues, that they were installed in the early twentieth century to spatially retain White supremacy. This story was told on empathic tours by Dr. Andrea Douglas and Jalane Schmidt in collaboration with local radio station WTJU.[10]

In August 2017, the weekend before the scheduled removal of the Robert E. Lee statue, hundreds of White nationalists and their supporters gathered in Charlottesville in what they called the Unite the Right rally. On August 12, the march became violent as protesters and counterprotesters clashed. James Alex Fields Jr. deliberately rammed his car into counterprotesters, killing Heather Heyer and injuring over thirty. Two state police troopers who were monitoring the events were killed in a helicopter crash.[11]

The aftermath of grief from the death, violence, and cultural division set a heightened context for the CMPJ. Virginia Senate Bill 183 and House Bill 1537 passed on July 1, 2020, allowing localities to remove or relocate monuments or war memorials. In Charlottesville, the *At Ready* Confederate soldier statue, installed in 1909 by the city, county, commonwealth, United Daughters of the Confederacy, and United Confederate Veterans, was removed on September 12, 2020.[12] The Stonewall Jackson statue, installed in 1921 on land confiscated by the city to remove McKee Row (a mostly Black-owned row of homes) in order to build an all-White school, was removed on July 9, 2021. The Jackson statue was removed the same weekend as the infamous Robert E. Lee statue from Market Street Park (formerly Lee Park), the focus of the 2017 Unite the Right rally.[13]

The Albemarle County Office of Equity and Diversity (ACOED) established the "Let's Talk Albemarle: Court Square" project in February 2020 as a hub for communications and public engagement to obtain feedback, asking how the public space could be intentionally programmed to tell a story about the city and what it values.[14] This project included panel discussions on expanding Black narratives at James Monroe's Highland and in "Court Square as a Public Space," a discussion in which I took part. Two community conversations were supported by a virtual tour of Court Square, generating twenty-six thousand responses on its comment board. The virtual tour explained the ACOED's in-depth research telling the true history of the statues and the historical markers defining White spatial narratives for Meriwether Lewis, Jack Jouett, Thomas Jefferson's Monticello plantation, and a Bicentennial Tribute installed in 1976 commemorating Thomas Jefferson, James Madison, and James Monroe, all of whom once frequented the courthouse. Each was placed under specific circumstances, without a cohesive master plan.

_mpathic design: The Process

In this section, I explain how we (the design team) used my _mpathic design process to reexperience Court Square and develop a design for the CMPJ.

Phase 1—Exploring

Tricia Hersey, founder of the Nap Ministry, tells us in *Rest Is Resistance* that "rest is anything that allow[s] your body and mind to connect in the deepest way." She states that rest "disrupts and makes space for invention, imagination, and restoration. Rest is an imagination tool because it makes space to simply be."[15] Hersey tells us that slowing down is one of the ways we can rest—and I apply this to the built environment. I started the first phase of my process by going to Court Square and slowing down to a meditative state to explore it. Exploring in this manner accesses what Hersey calls DreamSpace—"a well of knowledge, . . . a resting place for us to enter in to work things out."[16] Exploring accesses DreamSpace. I shared what I imagined in Court Square with the design team and community stakeholders, holding co-creative conversations to acknowledge a full history. This creates "feeling with," achieving what Professor LaToya Baldwin Clark explains: "We remember some things and forget others, and those things that we remember form our history, our stories, our understanding of who we are today. It is in our remembrance that we give those experiences power to push us forward as we interpret them to tell the story of our present. And the stories that we tell ourselves about our 'now' give us power to interpret the 'past' [so] as to see how it will all fit into our 'future.'"[17]

When the project started in the spring of 2019, Court Square's Confederate statues still stood. I repeatedly explored, holding interviews with community members while researching the ACOED's resources to deeply understand "in-feeling" to keep, remove, or contextualize Court Square's Confederate statues.

In these interviews, I learned new perspectives on how some residents appreciated Court Square's White spatial storytelling—and that some never really noticed it all. Essential to telling James's story in the square, I learned that in the Black community, the plantation aesthetics of the courthouse echoed accumulated realities of racial injustice by the city's judicial system.

To access DreamSpace while exploring, I asked questions to discover nuances, subtexts, undercurrents, and thoughts I noticed in Court Square. These questions get me thinking outside of myself.

What happened here? Who was here before me, us, now? Who once walked here? Why are these streets laid out the way they are? How old are these trees? What did this space look like untouched before the urban fabric was developed? Was corn grown here? Tobacco? Was this a plantation? Was there an overseer's house here?

Did the enslaved live here? Who were the Indigenous here? What are the reminders today that recall their story? Whose steps am I walking over? How did we get here? How do I understand what I see and what I don't? How do I feel being here? How do others feel? How should we remember? Do people feel comfortable here? What people? How can it feel comfortable for all?

I asked Siri Russell and staff at the ACOED for feedback on these questions while contacting local stakeholder groups, researching historical accounts, and reviewing the ACOED's "Let's Talk" resources. I wrote a descriptive account responding to the questions in journal format, incorporating the research, oral histories, and community conversations, and met with the design team to share again for feedback. An excerpt from the journal follows:

> Standing in the square amongst its massive Pin Oaks and blossoming Sweet Magnolia trees in late spring reminds you of Virginia's natural resources and agricultural histories, foundations of colonialist intention. You immediately feel small, dwarfed by nature. The slate, from nearby Buckingham County, appears, mounted under the front of the Court House, with a handwritten script stating that time starts in Charlottesville, Albemarle County, in 1762. Research and conversations tell you that there were once two city blocks here—one being the African American neighborhood of McKee Row.[18] But you would never know that today, no hints of its existence. In place of the Row is the Stonewall Jackson statue by famed sculptor Charles Keck, funded by Paul Goodloe McIntire.

I explored in the square repeatedly, getting deeper into DreamSpace, understanding its messiness, richness, and weightiness. To end this phase, the design team and I captured the experience in a collage, visualizing the forces surrounding the square and the feelings their architectures bring up for me and people of different backgrounds and histories (figure 7-1). I presented the collage to a local steering committee and advisory board, incorporating their feedback. The collage was so well received that it was installed as a mural at the city's Center for Community Partnerships in 2021. In 2022, the collage became the image for all marketing materials for the Equity Center's Starr Hill Pathways Summer Mentorship Program, with over one hundred local BIPOC (Black, Indigenous, and People of Color) students and twelve community organizations.

Figure 7-1: *DreamSpace Collage, Court Square* (concept credit: Tricia Hersey, *Rest Is Resistance*). Created with my design team (research and graphic support by My-Anh Nguyen, Gabriel Andrade, Abdureuf Hussien, Jake Johnson, Alissa Diamond, and Somrita Bandyopadhyay), the collage is currently installed as part of _mpathic design's work for the University of Virginia's Equity Center/Center for Community Partnerships. It was also used in the 2022 Starr Hill Pathways Program (executive director Ben Allen and Barbara Brown Wilson).

Phase 2—Uncovering the Layers

With the learnings from Phase 1, the design team and I analyzed what connections and extensions related to the untold narrative and asked, "How can the layers inform the design?" The layers are social, cultural, historical, economic, political, environmental, and natural. The design team and I discussed each layer, making notes as follows.

Social—We discussed how the square tells the story of White colonial society in every direction you look. It feels like surveillance if you're not White through its historical markers, Confederate statues, and plantation architecture of the courthouse. I shared how I feel as if I'm being watched in this public space, primarily from above. We discussed how images came to mind of the KKK rally that happened just a month before the Unite the Right rally.

Cultural—We discussed how the customs of Court Square are to come to this public space to honor colonial and Lost Cause histories and narratives to be passed down for generations. With the elevation of the square towering over the city's downtown, this honor radiates out in your subconscious, especially if you are a member of one of Charlottesville's marginalized communities.

Historical—We talked about the facade of the courthouse—which says that it was built in 1762. We shared how time is marked in the space, and 1898, the date of James's lynching, is etched along with his name on the front of the six-foot body column. I shared that I learned from the ACOED that the courthouse, designed by William Cabell in 1762, was also built by Black hands, by the bond of the enslaved laborers of John Fry, John Moore, and John Lewis, at 375 pounds, 10 shillings.[19] I shared that while I was exploring, an image came to mind from the city's historical archives of McKee Row.[20] I shared that as I walked around the corner of the courthouse to where the original city jail once was, I imagined what I'd read about the White lynch mobs in the alley between the buildings seeking to hang Black men awaiting their fate inside the jail.

Economic—We discussed that the marker for the Slave Market across the street to the southeast is horizontal, easy to miss within the brick sidewalk. I shared that while exploring, I imagined what you would have seen looking east from the square to the site of the Slave Market on top of the horizontal marker before turning around to where slave auctions took place in front of the courthouse.

Political—We talked about the informational panel on the right side of the courthouse stating that Thomas Jefferson called the courthouse "the common temple." James Monroe and James Madison (also slaveholders) frequented here, alternating between a place of worship by local churches and a meeting place for the KKK in the early 1900s.[21] I shared that while exploring, I imagined enslaved people being lashed in the gathering space in front of this common temple, at the public whipping post, or placed in the stocks or pillory for public humiliation.

Environmental—I explained that while exploring, I noticed that the blue-black slate on all of the surrounding buildings is from Buckingham County—and that Black hands quarried at Jefferson's Academical Village nearby. We discussed how uncomfortable I was at the National Memorial for Peace and Justice in Montgomery, that at the end of the memorial, you are standing underneath the body columns, which slowly rise until they are high above you to simulate a lynching. We discussed the color of the soil, the tree used for this act, and the feeling it would give to fellow citizens to be put in this position here in Court Square. We realized that it would make visitors think about the moments after John Henry James's lynching and the residue that would form on the ground from the rust-covered Corten steel body column if the blue-black slate made a platform underneath it. The soil from the lynching site matches the color of the rust.

Natural—I shared that I noticed how Court Square holds the highest elevation in downtown and that when looking southeast, you can see the rising ridge of Thomas Jefferson's Monticello. We talked about all the other plantations you would have seen from here. I noticed while exploring the massive pin oak trees in the southeast of the square and shared how they compete with the height of the statues and that I imagined echoes of Billie Holiday's "Strange Fruit" as the leaves rustled.

Phase 3—Mind, Hand, and Body

The design team and I took what we learned and discussed in the first two phases to create a conceptual design to share with the ACOED, community members in small groups, and one-on-one conversations for feedback. The _mpathic questions in this phase helped us critically analyze and deconstruct the CMPJ in Court Square to achieve "feeling with" the materials and spatial relationships we proposed.

In *Mind*, we thought about connections and extensions of self in the design.

> Is there a way to place the column and historical marker prompting visitors to the square to confront James's humanity and those who perpetrated the violence? How can the materials of the CMPJ help tell the story to visitors of all ages? How can the memorial be so accessible that even those walking by will want to come in to learn more? Can the CMPJ's spatial relationships hold space for grief? For joy? Remembrance? DreamSpace?

In *Hand*, we asked how the design could act as a catalyst to rethink the public space.

How can the design make people question the architecture of this public space and the systems that created it? How does the design put a mirror up to the public space?

In *Body*, we questioned the emotional impact of the design for the marginalized in the public space.

How does the design of the memorial make me feel? How does the design make others feel? Is the memorial inclusive? How can it change to be inclusive, and what are the values to incorporate? How does the design feel to someone who doesn't want to hear this story?

I've tested this process for over two and a half decades in academic, community, and professional contexts. It incorporates visitor experience methodology for global audiences from my sixteen years as lead designer at the Ontario Science Centre, one of Canada's most prominent public museums. Implementing Phases 1 and 2 in my Black male body has often created tense interactions with police and security guards and, at times in Court Square, with armed citizens "protecting" the statues. In this project (and in all of my work), I hold space to discuss these incidents to build trust with community to share their own experiences in the city's public spaces.

The Design

I remember that on my way to my first meeting with Siri Russell, the approach to Court Square from the strong grade up 4th Street NW was on axis with the Confederate soldier statue. But now, as you get closer to the plateau of the square, the statue is gone, and the empty patch of grass where it had stood since 1909 opens the front of the

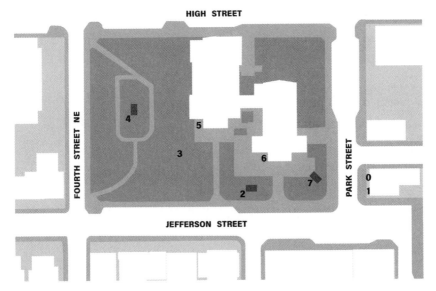

Figure 7-2: Site plan of Court Square and the CMPJ. (Drawing by My-Anh Nguyen with Elgin Cleckley) 0—the Number Nothing Building (former Mercantile Building); 1—former slave auction block; 2—Monticello historical marker; 3—former site of the Johnny Reb Confederate soldier; 4—former site of McKee Row; 5—former site of the Stonewall Jackson statue; 6—Albemarle County Courthouse; 7—EJI historical marker.

square like a terrace, allowing you to take in how magnificent its trees are (figure 7-2).

Past the patch of grass to the left is another patch of dirt where the Stonewall Jackson statue once was. This space is now an open square, and the benches stand out in the public space as never before, steps from the courthouse. I sit on one of the benches. With the statues removed, I can see clearly from one side of the square to the other as a breeze moves through with a cleansing effect. To my right is the courthouse, and just to the right is the six-foot body column monument etched with the name of John Henry James. The upright-mounted body column is strategically at grade (figure 7-3). This design gives off energy, and you think of James as you bring yourself face-to-face with it (this is what I heard from the ACOED, community members, and youth designers of our summer design mentorship program). You reach out and touch the rust on the front of the body column, looking down to notice it has left

Figure 7-3: Southeast view toward Thomas Jefferson's Monticello plantation. (Rendering by Gabriel Andrade with Elgin Cleckley)

Figure 7-4: West view of Court Square. (Rendering by Gabriel Andrade with Elgin Cleckley)

rust on the slate platform below. You look back up and see that the slate is all around you on nearby buildings. As you stand face-to-face with the column, you think back to how the statues hovered above. James is here, connecting with you in a form that meets you at a human height of six feet.

The rust of the body column evokes the act of the lynching between two large pin oak trees. As you turn back to the body column and look to the left, you see directly where the slave auction block was, just across the street and on the left, and a Monticello historical marker on the right.[22] The monitoring of the square through the Confederate soldier and Stonewall Jackson statues is gone—ghosts that you remember as you look around the square. As you continue to your left, the historical marker, designed by EJI, strategically places you in the axial direction toward Monticello. You read it and contemplate James's life then and your life today (figure 7-4).

Conclusion

My process stresses the importance of patience—that _mpathic design evolves from slowing down and connecting to a public space. This requires more time and budget in the conceptual and schematic phases. But it's needed to thoroughly generate _mpathic design with materials and spatial relationships that connect with community. The design was extremely well received, with community members stating how they felt that the body column being at grade brought James's humanity to light. Design adjustments included ensuring that a clear line of sight between the body column and EJI's historical marker would remain when large groups visited the memorial (figure 7-5). We were asked to provide clear visibility of the memorial from where the Stonewall Jackson statue once stood, which was planned to become a new public space after its removal. We also heard that in relationship to the historical marker,

Figure 7-5: Dedication Day for the Charlottesville Memorial for Peace and Justice (CMPJ) in Charlottesville's Court Square, July 12, 2019, 121 years after James's lynching. Siri Russell (in the center of the photo) stands where the body column is to be installed, delayed because of the COVID-19 pandemic. (Photo by Elgin Cleckley)

you found yourself looking around the square, making connections to the Slave Market, Monticello, and the locations where the Confederate statues once were. A community member told me that it "started a new, and necessary, conversation."

Earlier this summer, I walked up to Court Square, following the same path Jefferson took from Monticello in his phaeton, imagining that a Black man brought him here. As I walked around the square, I looked up to see a Black man, and we shared a hello. He was on the same bench where I had been deep in DreamSpace, reclining back in pure relaxation, looking toward the sky, just behind where the *At Ready* statue once stood, on axis with the CMPJ.

CHAPTER 8

Incorporating Empathy: To Middle Species, With Love, Columbus, Indiana

Joyce Hwang

FOR NEARLY TWO DECADES, I have been designing and building structures that are intended for inhabitation by nonhuman species. Often characterized as "animal architecture" or "habitecture," my projects create and amplify transspecies habitats and, more broadly, grapple with the built environment's crucial role in combating biodiversity loss. But how do we begin to design for—and with—animals? How do we consider the nature of nonhuman beings as stakeholders in our work? As a first step in my design processes, I often attempt to imagine the world through the lens of a project's inhabitants.[1] In selecting a site, for example, one could ask: Where might I, as a bird or a bat, want to take a break when scouting for food? Where is the closest body of water for proximity to hydration? In what kinds of spaces might I want to roost as a bat? As a small bird, where might I hide from predators?

In thinking through these sorts of projective questions, a useful concept to consider is the notion of the *Umwelt*, a term deployed by the late nineteenth-century biologist Jakob von Uexküll in describing the defining characteristics of specific environments that are significant to the inhabitants of that environment.[2] So, in other words, what are the conditions of a space that really matter, and to whom do they matter? As a biologist, Uexküll refers to an example regarding a tick and a deer. While both animals may be located in the forest, the *Umwelt*, or the specific environment for the tick, is not the forest but the deer itself. The forest matters to the deer, but it's the deer that matters to the tick. For a designer, the task of understanding and perhaps even embodying the *Umwelt* is an important part of the process in understanding what truly matters and for whom.

To illustrate an approach to empathic design, I will describe an installation that I developed for Exhibit Columbus,[3] an architecture biennial sited in Columbus, Indiana, that features public installations in the city's civic spaces. I was invited to be part of the 2020–2021 Exhibit Columbus cycle as university design research fellow. In response to the theme "New Middles: From Main Street to Megalopolis, What Is the Future of the Middle City?,"[4] my project, titled *To Middle Species, With Love*, aimed to amplify urban habitat conditions and draw awareness to the presence of urban wildlife in the Columbus region. In contrast to the notion of "flagship species"—in other words, the animals we as humans might think about when we consider wildlife conservation efforts, such as polar bears, rhinos, or other so-called charismatic species—"middle species" are those who are embedded in our environments and part of our everyday lives but often underacknowledged. Through design thinking and processes, how might we recognize them as our community members or neighbors?

Approach to Design

In foregrounding design for animals, I explore a number of gaps in the logic of "sustainability" as we have conventionally understood it. In the context of buildings, sustainability discourses have centered on issues such as electrification, renewable resources, weatherization and passive systems, and so on.

In the context of urbanism, conversations about sustainability tend toward strategies of resilience and green infrastructure. In thinking about our cities, we recognize that urban habitats—and the deleterious effects of habitat loss—are significant conditions to contend with, and we recognize flora and fauna for their significant roles in "ecosystem services," in other words, the role that ecosystems have in supporting human needs. Yet the role of animals—as sentient living beings—is often marginalized within current discourses of "sustainable design." How might we shift the consideration of animals beyond the scope of regulations, "services," and "performance"—to include agendas of spatial experience, care, ethics, and identity?

Acknowledging Animal Narratives and Lived Experiences through Research

To Middle Species, With Love is a project that aims to move the consideration of animals—our community members and neighbors—beyond ecosystem services and toward crafting spatial experiences that tap into empathy-driven sensibilities. To give a brief description of the project, the installation is a series of nine towers sited near the confluence of two rivers in Mill Race Park[5]—and adjacent to an iconic concrete observation tower. The nine structures are designed to support wildlife habitat—with bat houses and bird perches at the top and stone mounds for smaller terrestrial and amphibious animals at the ground. The bat houses are adaptations of a typical "rocket box" bat house design, which has been noted to be effective in serving as roosts for the endangered Indiana bat,[6] one of roughly thirteen bat species in Indiana. Several of the structures are equipped with bat detection equipment, which recorded bats' high-frequency echolocations—typically inaudible to the human ear—in and around the site each day and night.

Figure 8-1: *To Middle Species, With Love*, sited in Mill Race Park, near the observation tower. (Photo by Joyce Hwang)

This summary might be sufficient in explaining the performative motivations of the project as a functional ecological habitat project. But to move toward an empathic process that acknowledges and reflects on lived experiences and personal narratives—particularly in the case of urban wildlife—is, needless to say, a more complex and nuanced task.

What do animals say? How do we hear them? How do we know where they want to be and how they want to live? How do we understand their voices? And how do we do this when they are not easily visible or audible to us? While it is often the assumption that scientific inquiry doesn't necessarily lead to an adequate sense of empathy or subjective understanding, the role of scientific research—in the case of designing for animals—is critical in opening the window to a fuller understanding of our nonhuman neighbors. In my work, I typically consult with biologists and ecologists—as well as specialists such as entomologists. In the case of *To Middle Species, With Love*, I consulted with a mammalogist, Tim Shier, from the Indiana Department of Natural Resources to learn about bat species in Indiana and methods for tracking bats and to get a sense of where bats might "hang out," to think about siting the installation in a way to benefit and amplify bat habitats.

Yet the most poignant moments of the process emerged from a messier constellation of activities and conversations—not only with the biologists but also with artists, musicians, and environmental activists based in Indiana. I began discussions with several organizers from local nonprofits that had already been doing work in advocating for pollinators by transforming urban spaces into pollinator gardens, for example. Through these meetings, I learned about ongoing efforts in Columbus to support nonhuman flourishing. A transformative connection emerged from conversations with a local musician, Stuart Hyatt, who had—for many years—already been experimenting with recording sounds from the environment and bringing them into musical compositions. He had produced a project, titled *Ultrasonic*,[7] in which he worked with biologists to collect recordings of bats and use the sounds as source material for an album of songs, which was a collaborative process with many musicians. As I was thinking about and designing the installation project, I listened to Hyatt's *Ultrasonic* album on repeat. The songs are striking and evocative in how they foreground the bats' voices in each composition. One of the songs, titled "Between the Hawthorn and Extinction," is particularly powerful in how it combines an overlay of voices through both bat recordings (which we can hear through technology but not understand) and spoken word poetry (which we can understand). The recited poem, by Cecily Parks, offers glimpses into what bats might possibly say as they are out on their nightly journeys. Some poignant phrases in the piece are written as if the bats were speaking.

> My umbrella was cut in half says one.
> Goodbye havens and hibernacula says another.
> I never knew a belfry says one.
> I spent my whole life shouting hello says another.

Through our discussions, and inspired by Hyatt's music, I became even more compelled to explore the nightly lives of bats through first-hand listening experiences. In my research trip to Columbus, I made it an explicit point to spend time getting to know how bats, birds, and other animals inhabit the city through a series of hours-long walks. Carrying a number of ultrasonic detectors, bat recorders, and other wildlife recorders and listening through a pair of headphones, I meandered throughout the city—both day and night. Resulting from these walks were a collection of wildlife recordings, GPS-derived mappings of bat locations, and personal notations and observations, all of which became instrumental in the site selection process, as well as in developing the project design. Also emerging from these days of exploration was a confirmation of the emotive power of immersing oneself in the act of listening to voices and chatter between animals. Even if it is unintelligible to us, what's clear is that they live in community with one another.

Aesthetics and Care

A constant thread through my design projects is a concerted attention to aesthetics, morphology, and the resonances that are produced from the project's formal and spatial disposition. While attention to these issues might be considered to be a kind of formalism, I would argue that elevated attention to aesthetics, form, and space are crucial to prioritize in architectural projects, not only for the sake of design itself but also in projecting a sense of intentional care. All too often, in the instances where we find artifacts created in support of animals, we also find a projected sense of invisibility (a bat house that is tucked on the backside of a building or painted in such a way that it is camouflaged in among trees), or a reduced-effort aesthetic (why would we make an effort to have a nesting box look nice if animals don't care how it looks?). While it is arguable whether the aesthetics or formal disposition of an artifact may not be of importance to animals, I would argue that attention to these issues is important in projecting a sense of care and intentionality of design. As in the case of human communities, an elevated and intentional design contributes to a sense of dignity, as well as a perception of value. For communities of flora and fauna (particularly those that are less celebrated), this is significant in countering the tendency toward rendering them less visible. Architecture's role in addressing biodiversity enhancement and species conservation, therefore, is not only to consider the environment and ecosystem dynamics; it is also to focus on the formal and spatial design of artifacts and their aesthetics.

In a way, strategies for animal advocacy in architecture are not entirely different from strategies for animal conservation. Biologists use the term "nonhuman charisma" to describe the outward characteristics of species and the capacities of "charismatic" features to draw human interest and captivate hearts. In the case of architecture, it's the "character" of buildings and structures that becomes influential in conservation efforts.

The notion of aesthetic character is highlighted in *To Middle Species, With Love*. The structures were designed to respond to the adjacent observation tower—a stoic concrete structure with an observation deck at the top of the tower and extended space that reads as the tower's "head." Similarly, each of the installation's nine towers also has a "head," which is created from a series of wood planks that are layered to create gaps of bat inhabitation space. Rather than standing upright, however, the nine towers all lean toward one another in various directions. Some towers lean toward each other, almost appearing to be in conversation. Others lean toward a tower that is leaning in a different direction,

Figure 8-2: Dusk view. (Photo by Joyce Hwang)

Figure 8-3: Dry-stacked mound of stones, installation in progress. (Photo by Joyce Hwang)

appearing to be whispering to them or trying to get their attention. One senses perhaps that these towers are a grouping of characters in dynamic conversations.

Linked inextricably with aesthetic character is also the notion of craftsmanship and material consideration. In the case of *To Middle Species, With Love*, the decision to source local stones and to use species of wood that grow in Indiana was certainly a key driver in crafting the project's aesthetic disposition and effects. But in addition to that, an elevated execution of craftsmanship also connotes a sense of care—not only that it reflects care for the environment but also that it prioritizes those who inhabit it. In the case of this installation, my design team was particularly attentive to several considerations: first, using materials that would create an appropriately warm thermal environment for its potential inhabitants, and second, organizing the steel components and fasteners in such a way that sharp tips and edges remained embedded in wood, were covered, or were sanded down. An ongoing sentiment among the fabrication team was to always be on the lookout for conditions (such as protruding screw tips) where a bat wing might get accidentally caught.

Lessons Learned from "Testing" and "Prototyping" in the Design Process

While a consistent thread in my design projects is attention to craft and aesthetic resonance, another constant is addressing issues of environmental performance. In designing for flora and fauna, one of the questions I often encounter is "Does it work?" In nearly every discussion or conversation that I've had about my projects, inevitably someone asks whether I have seen animals living in my installations. Certainly, it is important to test this question throughout the process. In several of my projects, I have used visual and audio monitoring equipment—such as "camera traps" (motion-sensing cameras for wildlife documentation) and ultrasonic bat detection and recording equipment. This type of "post-occupancy" observation and documentation is crucial for broadening and deepening our knowledge about how animals inhabit the planet. But it's important to also acknowledge that the notion of "testing" does not end with the artifact or designed object itself but must necessarily always extend to its broader context. In the case of animal habitats, external environmental conditions always matter; temperature, humidity, light, shade, wind, proximity to water, access to food, and presence of predators are all equally significant to determining the suitability of any habitat.

In the case of *To Middle Species, With Love*, a particularly poignant moment of observation came even during the installation process itself.

While we were stacking the stones on-site, we noticed a number of very small toads trying to find their way into the stone mounds. Having sited the project near a river, and in an area of the park that was prone to flooding, we were expecting that amphibious species might find the stacked stones to be of interest, but we did not expect to see them attempting to take residence so soon. While observing these toads, we became aware that the height of the steel platform at the foundation made it a bit challenging for the toads to easily hop in. So, in response, we adjusted the design of the bases by adding stacked stone "steps" adjacent to each platform, which allowed for better access by smaller animals such as these toads.

Figure 8-4: A resident toad. (Photo by Joyce Hwang)

Further beyond the ecological context, how do we "test" a project's reception from the human perspective? This is where scientific inquiry overlaps with subjectivity. Although we as humans recognize the urgency to combat biodiversity loss and species extinction, as well as the importance of ecosystem services, our anthropogenic perception of urban animals is nonetheless conflicted. Depending on the situation at hand, animals are usually deemed to be a desired presence or seen as unwanted pests (why is it that we want to see birds in the park or in our backyards but not on our windowsills?). Since the perception of the urban "pest" is always contingent upon the proximal relationships between animals and humans, it is also critical for architecture and design to aid in advocating for our nonhuman coinhabitants of the planet. In this sense, small-scale installation projects hold the potential to serve as prototypes, not only to test and demonstrate ecological design principles, but also to shift and shape public perception about urban animals. The project—as a constructed urban animal habitat that amplifies wildlife conditions in

Figure 8-5: One of many tours led by Exhibit Columbus. (Photo by Hadley Fruits)

the city—has been part of a number of community-centered educational events, including tours for local K–12 students.

Collective Impacts and Responses

To Middle Species, With Love was conceived of and created as a temporary project for a design biennial, and in that sense, the project as it stands would not be able to truly serve as a long-term ecological testing site. As noted by our consulting biologists, the short-term periodic nature of biennials doesn't align well with the longer-term needs of ecological cycles. Yet—perhaps as a result of the collective public reception of the project during the Exhibit Columbus cycle—the installation will have the opportunity to live on and contribute to the community. Although the project is slated to be temporary by nature of its commission, it is—at the time of this writing—still standing in Mill Race Park after the conclusion of the exhibition period, owing to a request from the Indiana Department of Natural Resources (DNR) to keep the project in place for an additional year to continue monitoring. Additionally, I have been in conversation not only with the DNR but also with a local nonprofit organization, Friends of Pollinator Parks, about reinstalling the structures at different sites in the city to benefit their mission to amplify habitat for pollinators.

Beyond the built structures themselves, further impacts of the project have emerged from another interdisciplinary collaboration with sound artists. Inspired by the powerful effect of Stuart Hyatt's music, I commissioned two musicians, Shawn Chiki and Onokio (Zach Williams), to create soundtracks using the bat sounds gathered from the project's ultrasonic recorders as source material for electronic compositions.[8] For the opening of Exhibit Columbus, we premiered several of their pieces in a "bat concert." Also as part of the performance, two additional musicians (who also were part of Exhibit Columbus's team: graphic designer

Jeremiah Chiu and historian Enrique Ramirez) used the raw bat recordings as source material for live music performances. The enthusiastic reception of the idea of a "bat concert" began as early as the concept design presentation, when the idea was tossed into the Zoom chat by an audience member. The concert that took place during the opening of Exhibit Columbus received enthusiastic support as well, and it was—for me—a uniquely moving experience. Scheduled at dusk, we heard the sounds of the bats, modified and recomposed through electronic amplification, just as the bats were starting to emerge from a day's rest and populate the sky. The overlay of experiences was one that created a sense of both wonder and care for the environment, not only as an ecosystem but as a living community.

The public reception of animals as part of our community—and "deserving" of design attention and visibility—is a fundamental issue in my work to amplify transspecies habitats. All too often in our urban environments, appearances of "unregulated" flora and fauna are categorized as nuisances or lack of maintenance. This is a sentiment that needs to be addressed in how we design the built environment, particularly in the face of unprecedented biodiversity loss and mass extinction. While placing emphasis on the importance of ecosystem services is critical, I contend that it is equally critical to create experiences that intentionally evoke empathy. How can we design not only through empathic processes but also in a way that centers the role of empathy and its effects to radically shift our environmental narratives, to expand beyond our anthropocentric motivations and toward a more collective sense of care?

CHAPTER 9

Teaching Empathic Community Engagement Using Storytelling

C.L. Bohannon

As a classroom community, our capacity to generate excitement is deeply affected by our interest in one another, in hearing one another's voices, in recognizing one another's presence.

—bell hooks[1]

IT IS THE RESPONSIBILITY OF EDUCATORS to prepare students to think critically about social issues and to be intentional in their efforts to create a more just and equitable world. This responsibility is ever more apparent in design education as the history of design and planning disciplines has shaped physical, social, and environmental conditions through often harmful practices such as redlining, siting of hazardous industries in proximity to marginalized communities, and the demand for constant growth and development, which has led to displacement, homelessness, and ruptures in communities as well as in the built environment. Situated within the backdrop of systemic inequality and structural racism in America, there has been a call to action in institutions of higher education to respond more authentically to address the needs of the communities they serve. Often, the response from universities and educators materializes in some form of experiential learning opportunity. Overall, this work materializes in larger university-wide initiatives to do meaningful work to address community needs through outreach or service learning. In design fields such as landscape architecture, this work is done in community-engaged design studios, but it is not often done with the intentionality and care that is needed for it to be meaningful engagement. Too often, "community engagement" projects are done in problematic ways. Examples include work done in a community without community consent, use of extractive methods, and projects that do not address root issues of people's lived condition. A larger set of questions emerges as a result of such practices. First, in what ways are design responses unintentionally reproducing or reinforcing systemic issues such as marginalization, erasure, and neglect in the built environment, and how might more inclusive methods and practices intervene? And second, how are design educators preparing students to be intentional in their utilization of such methods as they become practitioners within the communities where they work and live?

I have committed in my scholarship and teaching to prepare students to be fearless in their pursuit of social and spatial justice by understanding and actualizing the power of empathy, narrative, and community engagement. This takes the form of developing the capacity to understand and relate to the feelings of another, engaging in storytelling and oral histories to gain appreciation of community histories and identities, and participating in sustained ways with communities to develop trust and reciprocal learning experiences. These processes encourage students and community members to engage with the pressing issues affecting their community. Through the core traits of empathy, narrative, and community engagement, it becomes possible to foster deep, meaningful, and long-standing connections between individuals, to develop shared understandings about the issues affecting communities (both in the classroom and beyond), and to create processes and spaces whereby people come together in celebration of their histories and visions for shared futures. In this chapter, I explore how empathy and narrative can be used to create meaningful and effective community engagement. I contextualize this by using a landscape architecture studio project that illustrates how empathic design can disrupt traditional practices in an effort to move toward empathically engaged work with people and spaces that requires the intentional pursuit of equity and justice.

Community Engagement

Community engagement, as it relates to higher education institutions, by definition is the "collaboration between institutions of higher education and their larger communities (local, regional/state, national, global) for the mutually beneficial exchange of knowledge and resources in a context of partnership and reciprocity."[2] American educator Ernest Boyer challenged institutions to rethink higher education completely by broadening the definition of scholarship to include discovery, integration, application, and teaching.[3] Boyer contended that universities need to develop partnerships with communities in order to afford transformative opportunities for change.

In its foundational report published in 1999, the Kellogg Commission, made up of the presidents and chancellors of twenty-five major public universities, acknowledged the historical role of higher education in serving the needs of the public and challenged educational institutions to renew their missions to address pressing societal issues. The resulting pedagogy driving forward this approach, known as "the engaged campus," has reshaped the way students learn and apply knowledge.[4] This approach is also present in design education and has altered traditional design approaches and the way design educators and students work with community members.

The methods landscape architects use in practice are inherently collaborative in nature, given that the nexus of our work aims to protect human and environmental health, safety, and well-being. Our practice requires us to work with clients, other designers, and community members from diverse backgrounds. It is important for landscape architecture and other design students to be exposed to real-life situations they will face as professionals. Collaborative learning through community engagement allows students to experience bringing together praxis, community engagement, and the design tools they have acquired. It is critical for students to develop professional capacities through education. Indeed, landscape architecture, as a professional degree, is "optimally positioned to integrate experiences where students learn through faculty role modeling to identify public need, accept responsibility to meet new challenges, and ultimately take action for meaningful societal change."[5] Integrating community engagement as a part of the educational process provides space for students to develop the values that will define their professional practice. Community engagement experiences help students develop a deeper understanding of their role in society and how to address societal needs.

This idea of social learning can be traced back to the work of educator and philosopher John Dewey, who was interested in learning that resulted from the relationship between people and their environment.[6] For Dewey, the interconnectedness of learning and doing could not be separated. He understood that the link between the process of learning, civic awareness through educational experiences, and reflexivity helped to provoke students' inquiry and curiosity about the world around them.[7] Dewey described three concepts of reflexivity—open-mindedness, responsibility, and wholeheartedness—that he saw as important to reflect in one's practice. Open-mindedness prepares a student to discover different points of view.[8] Responsibility involves the application of learned information from real situations to other circumstances. Finally, wholeheartedness enables students to evaluate issues critically to enact change in their environment.[9]

Philosopher Donald Schön stresses the importance of reflective practice through understanding the epistemology of practice and the ways practitioners do what they do.[10] As described by Schön, reflective practice is a "dialogue of thinking and doing."[11] Educational theorist David Kolb describes the process of experiential learning loops, whereby students go from experience to thought and back as they construct and organize the knowledge and meaning of their experiences.[12] Kolb's model, as shown in figure 9-1, starts with experience and moves to reflection, where students describe their experiences. From there, students go through a process of linking their experiential observations to other knowledge sources, which in turn generate questions that are tested through additional experiences.[13]

Figure 9-1: David Kolb's four-step experiential learning process. (Source: Institute for Experiential Learning, "What Is Experiential Learning? The Experiential Learning Cycle," https://experientiallearninginstitute.org/resources/what-is-experiential-learning/)

Empathy or Empathic Engagement

Empathy is the ability to understand and share the feelings of another person. It is different from sympathy, which is the ability to feel sorrow for another person's suffering. In design, empathy can be used to bridge the gap between designers and users, creating a space in which collaborative dialogue can take place. By understanding the needs of users, designers can create more effective and user-centered design proposals that center on various perspectives and experiences of users.

Empathy allows designers to connect with those we are engaging with on a personal level, which can help to foster better relationships and greater understanding. Developing empathy with members of a community helps educators and students gain insight into their unique perspectives and experiences, allowing us to create more effective strategies for meaningful dialogue. Empathy encourages active listening skills that allow people to be heard and understood, leading to improved communication and stronger relationships between different stakeholders. By using empathic principles when engaging with communities, it is possible to create mutual trust and respect, which can lead to fruitful collaboration during the community engagement process.

Urban planner Leonie Sandercock calls this the "epistemology of multiplicity," and central to this ethos is the importance of dialogue and listening.[14] Sandercock asserts that this type of work "suggests an entirely different practice in which communicative skills, openness, empathy, and sensitivity are crucial; in which we respect class, gender, and ethnic differences in ways of knowing, and actively try to learn and practice those ways in order to foster a more inclusive and democratic planning."[15] In community-based practice, it is important to listen to residents, but it is equally important to be able to ask the right questions. Listening can help students gain credibility when working with community members. Attuned listening can help students get to root issues and begin to understand how power relations work within a community.[16] Judith Innes and David Booher argue that local knowledge is critical for social justice and resilience in our communities.[17] Local knowledge provides a grounded context and fills in gaps of missing information. Community engagement projects often involve working with people from different backgrounds and cultures and require an understanding of the local needs and concerns of the community. Empathy is an important skill for designers to have because it enables them to create better design solutions that are more responsive to the needs of communities.

The Power of Storytelling

Stories play an important role in the development and survival of cultures. Stories provide information about language, history, and the environment and can be in written form or in verbal form, such as oral histories and folk music. Stories and histories are connected in our daily lives and contribute to the makeup of our society, from local communities to entire cities. It is important for designers to understand that knowledge does not rest solely in higher education but exists outside of the boundaries of institutions.

Within design fields, we have only scratched the surface of the power of stories to progress justice and equity. Sandercock writes, "In order to imagine the ultimately un-representable space, life, and languages of the city, to make them legible, we translate them into narratives."[18] She makes the case that planning and design practice is performed through stories and draws upon knowledge from multiple starting points, including the social sciences, humanities, and art. The use and understanding of stories for design students can lead to increased critical thinking and richer understanding of the built environment, but we must be critical of the meaning and origin of stories and how power plays a role in which stories are told. For example, it is important to provide space for community members to tell and center their stories in community development processes rather than have someone telling their stories to frame community change.

Stories can be the foundation for change and provide new imaginings of the world around us. Dominant cultures normally play significant roles as to which stories are recognized. This is also the case in landscape architecture, given that over 80 percent of professionals identify as White; in urban planning, approximately 67 percent as White; and in architecture, 65 percent as White. Within a multicultural context, it is important to challenge the norms and not be afraid to tell stories of shock and surprise, including the ways in which we educate our students to work in more collaborative and equitable ways. One method that I use in my community engagement process and studio pedagogy is collecting oral histories. An oral history is more than an interview to uncover facts about the past; it has the power to force us to reconcile meanings and interpretations within memories.[19]

Oral histories are conversations, often through interviews, between people to gather and preserve the voices or memories of a community. It is these complexities between people, mainly having a human participant, that provide this method with unique opportunities for analysis and interpretation. First, a person cannot be analyzed in the same way as a document or picture. Oral histories are a dialogic process between an interviewer and narrator and the narrator and external discourses.[20] These external discourses are related to our culture, life webs, and environment.

Within community-engaged processes, genuine dialogue, which emphasizes listening and shared understanding, can be an important link to resolving conflicts and developing relationships between residents and community partners. Dialogue can help people develop a holistic understanding of their own experiences and how they relate to a larger collective community identity. This is what Donald Schön calls frame reflection, in which a person can act from one viewpoint but also be able to look through a different lens for other possibilities.[21] At its root, dialogue is a process that transforms our thinking process, in which we abandon our own position as final. Genuine dialogue should be creative and focused on learning and transformation as well as action. In practice, dialogue should not be focused on winning and losing but rather on exchanging knowledge.

Stories are a powerful tool for fostering empathy in design education because they can help bridge the gaps between people from different backgrounds. By sharing stories and experiences with others, we create a sense of shared understanding that allows us to relate to other people's perspectives on an emotional level. This helps build stronger relationships and encourages collaboration between students who may be coming from vastly different contexts or worldviews. Storytelling can also help bring together diverse voices to work toward solutions that benefit everyone involved, increasing the potential for more meaningful outcomes in design projects.

Case Study: The Hill, Apalachicola, Florida

In the spring of 2020, a team of community members, designers, educators, and documentary filmmakers were awarded a Mellon Foundation grant to begin a three-year initiative to recover and celebrate local Black history, improve community well-being, and mitigate displacement pressure of the Hill community, which is located in Apalachicola, Florida. Locally known as Apalach, this community of two thousand residents is located on Highway 98 along Florida's Forgotten Coast. The Hill's location along the Forgotten Coast comes with its challenges: the community has experienced a loss of its cultural expression, which centers the question of who and what communities have been forgotten along the coast.

The Hill, Apalachicola's historically Black neighborhood, continues to be a tight-knit community despite being erased from the city's official history. The Hill was a lively neighborhood with family houses, a thriving business district, a Black high school, and numerous churches and fraternal groups that all contributed to a broader social life as recently as the 1960s. After the 1960s, the community faced economic hardships and a loss of population as people moved to other communities. Currently, the Hill is in danger of property loss through vacancy and gentrification, with few employment opportunities in the area as a result of decades of economic underinvestment and the demise of the fishing industry. As of 2023, on the Hill, there are about seventy-five unoccupied residences in various conditions from abandoned to uninhabitable. Other residences have been bought and repaired by recent arrivals to the neighborhood, who frequently are recent arrivals to the city and whose presence is fueling gentrification.

Stemming from student, faculty, and alumni calls for action, in the fall of 2023, as part of a schoolwide justice, equity, diversity, and inclusion initiative at the University of Virginia, the core studio III in the Masters of Landscape Architecture program was redesigned to incorporate community-engaged design pedagogy as a core component of student learning and experience. The goal of the studio was to develop a regional atlas, cultural asset maps, and community design strategies with techniques transferable to other communities affected by structural racism. The teaching team focused on grassroots storytelling and capacity building to center the voices of residents of the Hill in design decision-making processes in a complex and fragmented policy landscape. Thirty-five students worked alongside residents of the Hill community in Apalachicola. The students were charged with engaging with residents to produce work that countered historical practices of marginalization that shape the spatial, economic, and environmental conditions that have proven problematic to Black communities. The studio was centered on intentional community engagement through unpacking of personal histories and stories of community members in an effort to build students' empathic capacity and develop more inclusive design practices.

The studio was divided into three modules. In the first module, students were asked to unpack the interwoven relationships between narrative, identity, story, and histories at various scales. To start these exercises, the teaching team, composed of three faculty members, asked students to develop their own deep map situating their own identity and narrative through a layered palimpsest of people, community, and place. This prepared students to be in a vulnerable position, much as community members are when participating in community engagement processes.

First, the students were asked to work together to develop a series of questions to guide an oral history interview. For example, questions centered on where students grew up and in what ways community and place had shaped their worldview. Students then paired up and interviewed each other using the questions. The students used the responses of their partners to develop a deep map through the layers of people, community, and place as a representation of their oral histories, interviews, and personal reflections, as shown in figure 9-2.

In the second module, students were asked to develop atlases with maps showing the evolution, structure, and cultural complexities of the region. The goal was to investigate and develop a map that made visible structural inequalities that impacted residents of the Hill. The hope was that students would apply what they had learned about how people, place, and community are intertwined to a place they did not know personally. Students were given a few guiding questions for this assignment to get them started. First, "What is the narrative in this region that you are making visible?," and second, "What is uneven about the geography that should be revealed?" Examples of student maps included the relationship between slavery and ecological exploitation, as shown in figure 9-3; media narratives of hurricanes; and the plight of the longleaf pine. These maps helped students understand how the history of the region has shaped its current challenges and opportunities.

Figure 9-2: Yichen Wan's deep map illustrates how people, place, and community map onto her life experiences. (Credit: Yichen Wan, MLA student, University of Virginia)

The third module focused on community asset mapping and included a four-day studio visit to the Hill in the fall of 2023. Students were asked to work with community members through a participatory mapping approach to develop cultural asset maps that centered on twenty-one historic sites in the Hill. Students began by conducting field research on the community-identified sites. They collected oral histories of community members to restore a sense of belonging in the community and to educate the broader public in Apalachicola about the people, places, and experiences of the Hill. This assignment gave

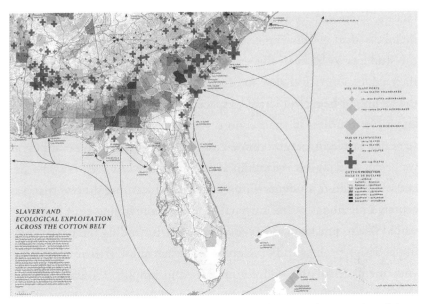

Figure 9-3: Celina Qiu's map illustrates the relationship between the institution of slavery and ecological exploitation in the American South. (Credit: Celina Qiu, MLA student, University of Virginia)

students an opportunity to understand the importance of community history by extending their education beyond the traditional limits of the classroom. This assignment challenged and reversed the ordinary roles of educator and student, community member and design professional. The engagement and mapping process emphasized that knowledge held by community members was more valuable to situate a just and equitable future for the Hill than traditional "objective" data sources. Only when designers possess the humility to pause and listen to the insights of the community members can design as a discipline become a force for justice and empowerment.

The studio team developed personal deep maps, regional atlases, community asset maps, and community development strategies with techniques transferable to other communities impacted by structural racism. There were a number of impacts on students and community members during this project. First, there was some resistance from the students to learn in this engaged way that centered their voices in their education. I feel that the resistance to the pedagogy was due to the feeling of being vulnerable, especially when the vulnerability could be visible to others in their cohort. As we developed trust through the semester, students became more comfortable with the vulnerability as we began to establish the studio as a community of co-learners. By the end of the studio, students found the engaged learning process that was centered on empathy and storytelling to be more in line with how they would like to practice landscape architecture by finding their own voice in the design process and developing skills that allowed them to connect with members of the Hill community and amplify the community's needs in their work. For members of the Hill community, the work the students produced during the semester gave them a fresh look at a place they knew. The students were able to work with the shared narratives, site visits, and conversations to develop proposals that will assist the community in developing strategies that tie into the cultural assets and future visions of the Hill. I think this type of community engagement studio is one example of how to put into action principles of justice, equity, and inclusion in design education where students will be able to carry this way of working with them into the profession. Overall, this studio experience provided an opportunity for this studio cohort to connect their place-based experiential learning experience to the epistemological why and how the practice of landscape architecture can be transformative in community engagement projects.

Conclusion

Stories provide a unique and powerful perspective in which the issues that affect community members can be understood. When used properly, stories can create a shared understanding of the community's struggles. This shared understanding helps stakeholders feel connected to one another and more passionate about resolving any issues or challenges present.

Narrative-based engagement strategies allow designers to create a shared language that can be used in conversations about difficult issues. This common language builds trust between stakeholders because individuals with different backgrounds and ages can easily understand and relate to these stories. Further, sharing stories allows us to better empathize with one another, which strengthens our resolve when facing difficult situations together as a community. By leveraging narrative in community engagement efforts, community groups have the potential to foster meaningful dialogue and stronger relationships between stakeholders while still addressing critical problems. Being part of these community processes is paramount in the development of designers who understand how to utilize their skills to work with community stakeholders in an informed and nonextractive manner.

Planning with Purpose:
Repairing Past Harm with Empathy

Mitchell J. Silver

IT IS SUCH A PRIVILEGE TO BE PART OF AN IMPORTANT BOOK at this point in history. The aftermath of the Black Lives Matter movement has forced some Americans to reflect on their country's centuries of systemic racism and the generational trauma it inflicted. It is my hope that this book challenged you not only to think differently but to act differently as well. Elgin Cleckley's introduction to this book is shaped by his perspective as a Black man, and it frames empathic design in a clear, understandable way. He eloquently explains how empathic design challenges us to be empathic designers in practice. As a reminder, Elgin wrote that "empathic design is part of the design justice movement" and that it "offers communities the opportunity to acknowledge the full history of a place and engage in a healing design process through planning for future uses that engage and embrace everyone in a community."

I also appreciate the diverse group of contributing authors, who shared examples of the empathic design approach to reveal the joy, pain, grief, trauma, memories, stories, and healing, by the simple act of listening and understanding how people feel. The primary takeaway of this book is that empathy must be at the center of the planning and design process. As planners and designers, we must attain the ability to understand how other people feel in a situation from their point of view, rather than our own.

Planning for Place, Planning for People

As a planning student in graduate school, I was very fortunate to find my sense of purpose at a young age—well, at the age of thirty-three. The first inspiration came while I was working on a studio project in Central Harlem while attending Hunter College's Urban Planning Program in New York City. As I walked the streets of Harlem, a powerful insight overcame me. Planning is about place, but more important, it is about people. I am not the first planner to reach this conclusion, but I was determined at that point in my life to center my planning career on people. Rather than be fixated solely on land use, zoning classifications, building condition, and neighborhood character, I wanted to learn about the soul of the community, the people's experiences, physical and mental well-being, local customs and culture, past and present trauma, memories, and sacred gathering places. I wanted to learn by observing and listening to people and not solely focus on site visits, data collection, and surveys. I needed to listen to understand how community members felt about past or present events from their viewpoint. To be a great planner, I knew I had to learn how to listen with empathy.

I also knew my approach was not common, but I was given the opportunity to share my perspective in *Local Planning: Contemporary Principles and Practice* by the International City/County Management

Association (ICMA). I wrote about "the anatomy and soul of a place"[1] because I wanted planners to consider a role apart from the traditional one we were taught in planning school. Rather than analyzing land use patterns and the built environment, I wanted planners to see themselves as doctors, detectives, and evangelists who can help heal a community. In other words, planners should be guardians, healers, and protectors. In retrospect, I should have added empathic listeners and observers. I have held on to my sense of purpose from graduate school to my current position today, and I have witnessed firsthand the lasting impact that embracing a sense of purpose can have on a community when you humbly approach your mission with empathy.

Lead and Inspire with Purpose: Code of Ethics

As a former president of the American Planning Association (APA) and immediate past president of the American Institute of Certified Planners (AICP)—the first Black person to serve in both roles—I have always been inspired by the AICP Code of Ethics and Professional Conduct. As a curious planner, I have read the codes, charters, and canons of other allied professions, but I remain inspired by the AICP Code of Ethics. Why? The AICP code is intentional as it relates to social and racial issues. Those engaged in planning should aspire to five overarching principles: (1) people who participate in the planning process shall continuously pursue and faithfully serve the public interest; (2) people who participate in the planning process shall do so with integrity; (3) people who participate in the planning process shall work to achieve economic, social, and racial equity; (4) people who participate in the planning process shall safeguard the public trust; and (5) practicing planners shall improve planning knowledge and increase public understanding of planning activities.[2] What inspires me most about the code are the points listed under principle number 3 (emphasis added):

3. People who participate in the planning process shall work to achieve economic, social and racial equity.

a. Create plans that ensure equitable access to resources and opportunities which, in turn, structure prospects for upward economic mobility, *a sense of belonging*, and an enhanced quality of life. *Recognize our unique responsibility to eliminate historic patterns of inequity* tied to planning decisions represented in documents such as zoning ordinances and land use plans.

b. Seek social justice by identifying and working to expand choice and opportunity for all persons, emphasizing our special responsibility to plan with those who have been marginalized or disadvantaged and to promote racial and economic equity. *Urge the alteration of policies, institutions, and decisions that do not help meet their needs.*

c. *Recognize and work to mitigate the impacts of existing plans and procedures that result in patterns of discrimination, displacement, or environmental injustice.* Plan for anticipated public and private sector investment in historically low-income neighborhoods to ensure benefits defined by the local community. Promote an increase in the supply and quality of affordable housing and improved services and facilities with equal access for all residents, including people with disabilities.

d. Promote the inherent rights of indigenous people and work with indigenous peoples on developments affecting them and their lands and resources.[3]

These principles look great on paper, but exactly how could the code of ethics be applied in practice? Can these aspirational principles be achieved without empathy for those we are planning and designing for? How do we use empathic design to address or repair past harm or historical patterns of inequity?

Repairing Past Harm

The planning profession is finally coming to terms with its role in unjust practices regarding communities of color. In September 2021, planning directors of twenty US cities "released a joint public statement to collectively address racial equity issues in their practices and policies, with a commitment to change their work toward the goal of racially equitable communities in the future. The statement acknowledges decisions that have undermined equity in the past that are directly and indirectly attributable to planners, noting that these policies and actions negatively impacted the quality of neighborhoods and communities of color, and are related to aspects of current planning work."[4]

In January 2022, I shared my thoughts on the new revisions to the code that went into effect on January 1, 2022. The code was revised to include a greater emphasis on social equity, among other changes. In the article, "Lead and Inspire with Purpose: AICP Code of Ethics Update,"[5] I summarized the revisions to the AICP Code of Ethics and underscored that the APA and AICP strongly believe these revisions urge planners to account for their role in social justice and racial equity, to respect the rights of others, and to increase opportunities for underrepresented groups to become professional planners. Addressing past harm is not just the right thing to do; it is our professional obligation as planners. Planners and designers must recognize our unique responsibility to eliminate historical patterns of inequity tied to planning decisions represented in documents such as zoning ordinances and land use plans.

In April 2023, I and a team of planners presented a topic, we believe for the first time, at the APA's National Planning Conference, which that year was held in Philadelphia, Pennsylvania, and titled "Repairing Past Harm: Do Planners Have a Role?" The room was packed, for either educational purposes or pure curiosity.

The session underscored the aspirational part of the code of ethics and planners' professional obligation to address past harm. We gave an overview of reparations in the United States and then shared practices from federal, state, and local governments addressing a historical injustice. Since planners and designers have minimal influence in enacting reparations or appointing a commission or a task force to examine the impact of past harm, what is a planner's role in addressing or repairing past harm?

We shared a list of unjust practices, past and present, and urged those in attendance to add to this list, because by no means is the list exhaustive.

Unjust Planning Practices Past and Present

- Enslaved labor
- Redlining
- Segregation
- Jim Crow
- Urban renewal plans
- Use of eminent domain to build large-scale developments, infrastructure, and highways
- Racially motivated and discriminatory public policies, rules, regulations, laws, and ordinances
- Restrictive covenants
- Exclusive single-family zoning districts
- Racial profiling
- Antidensity measures
- Exclusively designed public spaces
- Uneven code enforcement
- Purchase of real estate and heirs' property through predatory practices
- Displacement

I attended a diversity summit in California in the fall of 2022 to gain a deeper understanding of how that state is addressing past harm. In 2020, California became the first state in the country to establish a state reparations task force, and in 2022 the panel released its first report outlining the state's involvement in slavery and how it continues to harm Black Americans.[6] One speaker shared three important steps to take in repairing past harm: acknowledge, apologize, and atone. The speaker went on to name cities in California that had publicly issued a resolution apologizing for past harm, such as Glendale and San Francisco, the latter of which is considering "payments of $5 million to every eligible Black adult, the elimination of personal debt and tax burdens, guaranteed annual incomes of at least $97,000 for 250 years and homes in San Francisco for just $1 a family."[7]

As stated earlier, planners and designers do not have the influence or power to enact reparations or to appoint a commission or task force to examine the impact of past harm. Therefore, I have developed a list of approaches and tools to serve as a first step.

Approaches and Tools for Planners and Designers to Use to Address Past Harm

- Apologize at the beginning of the public engagement process for harm created by the planning profession.
- Listen with empathy and go on a walking tour to observe the harm in person.
- Conduct a study to understand the implications of past harm.
- Undertake an equity audit or assessment at the beginning of the planning or design process.
- Undertake an audit of the zoning code and planning documents and ordinances to identify harmful rules, policies, or practices.
- Suggest a new methodology for selecting capital projects that is more just and equitable.

- Examine the names of streets, public buildings, and public spaces and monuments.
- Identify sacred sites and buildings that may not fit the traditional historic preservation criteria.
- Identify funds to offer grants for housing rehabilitation or down payments.
- Suggest tax relief or a homestead exemption.
- Eliminate or encourage adopted urban renewal areas to sunset.
- Suggest the decision-making body to explore reparations legislation or create a commission or task force to study past harm.
- Recommend a racial equity fund to support underserved communities.
- Advocate for funding to repair urban renewal scars created by erasure of neighborhoods, large-scale developments, highways, and other infrastructure projects.

An Empathic Design—Juneteenth Grove

During the summer of 2020, at the height of the COVID-19 pandemic, George Floyd's brutal murder shocked the world. Most people may not recall, but earlier that same day, Christian Cooper, a Black bird-watcher, confronted a White woman in Central Park who had her dog off leash in a restricted area of the park. Rather than apologize and restrain her dog, the woman called 911 and pretended she was being harassed by a Black man. Christian recorded the event on his phone, and within hours the video went viral. As commissioner of the New York City Department of Parks and Recreation (NYC Parks), I was notified of the event as soon as the video went live. I contacted my communications team to prepare for press inquiries. A few hours later, the news of George Floyd's murder broke and dominated the news cycle.

Watching the video of the murder on the news was extremely

painful. After years of checking my Black identity at the door, I finally concluded that enough is enough. I am grateful for the passion, courage, and determination of the younger generation as they protested for giving me the courage to be more intentional and outspoken about the topic of race. After careful contemplation, I decided to share a message with my staff on June 1, 2020. For me, it was an awakening to have deeper empathy for those who have been harmed and traumatized for being a person of color.

I will never forget what my White friends, colleagues, and allies asked me as they watched the protests and social unrest unfold on national news. "What can I do?" I paused and politely responded, "That is the wrong question. Do not ask me what you can do; ask me, your friends, your colleagues, 'How do you feel?'" Asking me what you can do is about *you*. Asking me how I feel is about *me*. They were well-intentioned but showed no empathy. They did not understand how we felt after the trauma of watching a man being murdered before our very eyes as he cried out for his deceased mother to rescue him. You cannot help in these situations unless you have empathy, and that empathy must be at the center of repairing past harm and at the center of the planning and design process. As previously stated, we planners and designers must acquire that ability to understand how another person feels in a situation from their point of view, rather than our own.

In the days following George Floyd's murder, I decided to hold virtual calls with staff. We named the calls "Reflections." The first round of calls was for Black staff only. The next round of Reflections was open to all staff. The purpose of Reflections was simple—it was intended to be a safe space to share how staff members felt. They could be anonymous, with audio only, or share their video. They could speak or just listen. As head of the agency, I shared first. After I spoke, staff shared powerful and painful emotions. One Parkie (a nickname for a parks department employee) commented on the message I had shared with staff a few days prior. They urged me to share my message publicly. I agreed.

Dear Parkies,

This is a difficult, but necessary message to write.

Compounded by what we have been experiencing during the COVID-19 crisis—isolation, illness, and loss and grief—in real time, we are watching unfold before our very eyes the impact that stifled rage can have on a community that has experienced generations of systemic racism.

Triggered by the recent killings of George Floyd, Ahmaud Arbery and Breonna Taylor, and the false assault accusations against Christian Cooper, across New York City, the state, the country, and around the world, people are rallying together, crying out in despair—demanding change.

What we are seeing in parks and streets are protests with two personalities; peaceful protests and those hijacked by people inciting violence, creating chaos and wreaking havoc. Some of what is unfolding is a direct result of the unleashed pain, anger and rage one feels having lived in an unjust society, hurt by racism and discrimination. The balance, the worst of it, is inflicted by the same people who are infiltrating to cause more damage.

I know that what is happening around us is causing many of you the same kind of anguish that it is causing me. When issues of race and pain well up, it's like a scab being ripped off and we are forced to address feelings we have pushed way down inside— based on what we have personally experienced and what we have witnessed—just to get by.

As a Black Man and the head of this agency, one of my goals is to make sure that NYC Parks is diverse and a safe space for all. That we walk-the-walk, and not just talk. That we protect and respect

Parkies regardless of your color, creed, gender identity, race, and religion. So that we can serve the people of New York City, providing them with greenspaces where they can cultivate community and enhance their physical and mental health.

Because of my role and these occurrences, I am reflecting on my life, experiences and suppressed emotions related to the racism, prejudice, and unconscious bias I have faced personally and professionally. And, I hope you are too.

As you reflect and cope with what is going on in your life and in the world around you, I want you to know that Parks has resources in place to help you address any related concerns.

I want you to also know, we are working to provide other resources and experiences for Parkies that will address systemic racism and the resulting repressed rage. I am hopeful that through dialog and doing, that just like the graffiti, damaged property and defaced monuments will be cleaned and repaired, that our emotional scars can be soothed, nurtured and healed, so we all can live equitably.

Thank you and see you in the parks.

Sincerely,

Mitchell Silver, FAICP

Commissioner, NYC Parks

After a series of Reflections, staff asked me what the parks department could do to show solidarity with the Black Lives Matter movement. I came up with the idea of elevating the Black experience in New York City by creating a space for reflection, joy, meditation, protest, and celebration—a place of belonging. That is how Juneteenth Grove was conceived[8]—by listening first and acting later. Juneteenth Grove is an empathic design that is simple but powerful.

After searching for a location throughout the parks system, we narrowed down the search to two locations. My instructions were simple—the site had to have special meaning. I sent out a senior member of my team to visit Cadman Plaza Park in Downtown Brooklyn, which happened to be the location of protests. The Brooklyn parks commissioner called and said, "Boss, you won't believe it. There are nineteen benches at the entry of the park." One year before Juneteenth became an official holiday, I renamed a portion of Cadman Plaza Park "Juneteenth Grove." We painted the nineteen benches the Pan-African colors of red, black, and green. We planted nineteen rosebud trees, and we created official park signs and banners.

Figure A-1: Juneteenth Grove. (Credit: Mitchell J. Silver)

Figure A-2: Cadman Plaza. (Credit: NYC Parks)

Figure A-3: Woman painting bench. (Credit: NYC Parks)

Staff painted the benches and planted the trees. I planted one of the trees and prayed in front of the tree to honor our ancestors, as well as for future generations that may experience this space. Juneteenth Grove was created for visitors to reflect, feel joy, protest, and feel a sense of belonging. I will never forget the day Juneteenth became an official holiday. Leading up to June 19, 2021, the parks department was getting multiple calls for elected officials and community groups to obtain a permit to hold an event at the grove. I had a hunch that whether or not we issued a permit to use the space, people would be going to Juneteenth Grove to celebrate the new national holiday. I passed Juneteenth Grove that day after returning from a Juneteenth 5K race at a nearby park. I stopped and sobbed at what I saw. As I predicted, the grove was packed and overflowing with visitors. It was like a reunion—a homecoming. But what was most profound was the joy people were expressing. Black joy. So many people were drawn to that space because they felt a sense of belonging. This place is special. *I belong here.*

Figure A-4: Mitchell J. Silver blessing the newly planted grove. (Credit: NYC Parks)

Conclusion

My hope is that you will share the wisdom you have absorbed in this book on empathic design as well as impart the perspectives and examples on creating empathic spaces to others. Our hope is that this book will change the way you think and act as you design and plan spaces and places for people now and in the future.

Notes

Introduction

1. "Lynching of John Henry James (1898)," *Encyclopedia Virginia,* accessed February 9, 2022, https://encyclopediavirginia.org/entries/lynching-of -john-henry-james-1898-the/.

2. "Lynching of John Henry James."

3. "Lynching of John Henry James."

4. Brendan Wolfe, "The Train at Wood's Crossing," accessed November 24, 2021, http://brendanwolfe.com/lynching.

5. Equal Justice Initiative, "Community Remembrance Project," accessed May 18, 2023, https://eji.org/projects/community-remembrance-project/.

6. Rebecca Solnit, *Recollections of My Nonexistence: A Memoir* (London: Penguin Books, 2020), 110.

7. Karla McLaren, *The Art of Empathy: A Complete Guide to Life's Most Essential Skill* (Boulder, CO: Sounds True, 2013), 4, ix.

8. Sasha Costanza-Chock, *Design Justice: Community-Led Practices to Build*

the Worlds We Need, Information Policy Series (Cambridge, MA: MIT Press, 2020), 7.

9. These points were received in feedback from community officials after an online lecture about _mpathic design I gave to the Virginia Department of Housing and Community Development (DHCD) as part of its Creating Community Vitality Series, October 13, 2021.

10. Cleckley, lecture to DHCD.

11. Robert Lamb Hart, "Architectural Empathy: Why Our Brains Experience Places Like People," *Metropolis*, June 30, 2016, https://metropolismag .com/projects/architectural-empathy-why-our-brains-experience-places -like-people/. See also Robert Lamb Hart, *A New Look at Humanism: In Architecture, Landscapes, and Urban Design* (Novato, CA: ORO Editions, 2016).

Chapter 1. From Empathy to Ethics

1. George Aye, "When Design and Ethics Collide," talk given at Brainstorm Design 2022 conference, May 24, 2022, https://fortune.com/videos /watch/Brainstorm-Design-2022--Design-Talk-that-Quiet-Little-Voice --When-Design--Ethics-Collide/026f03d0-20f1-4174-97d0-4584942 fae24.

2. *Cambridge Dictionary*, s.v. "empathy (*noun*)," accessed November 28, 2022, https://dictionary.cambridge.org/us/dictionary/english/empathy.

3. *Merriam-Webster*, s.v. "empathy (*noun*)," accessed November 28, 2022, https://www.merriam-webster.com/dictionary/empathy.

4. Personal notes from my meeting with NYC Health + Hospitals/Bellevue Program for Survivors of Torture (PSOT), 2017.

5. Aye, "When Design and Ethics Collide."

6. This paragraph draws from Sharon Salzberg's book *Real Change: Mindfulness to Heal Ourselves and the World* (New York: Flatiron Books, 2020), including a passage on page 128 in which she quotes the work of Tania Singer.

7. Gaspar, notes from meeting with PSOT.

8. Public Policy Lab, "New View of Consent," Medium, June 11, 2021, accessed December 1, 2022, https://public-policy-lab.medium.com/new -view-of-consent-3958e6900eb3.

9. Sara Cantor Aye, Greater Good Studio, "The Gut Check," Medium, May 27, 2016, updated February 27, 2019, accessed December 1, 2022, https://medium.com/greater-good-studio/the-gut-check-work-better-and -happier-by-formalizing-your-feelings-fe76a9854c2e.

10. Design Justice Network, "Design Justice Network Principles," accessed December 1, 2022, https://designjustice.org/read-the-principles.

Chapter 2. Making Space for Grief

1. Allison Arieff, "Where Are All the Female Architects?," *New York Times*, December 15, 2018, accessed December 10, 2022, https://www.nytimes .com/2018/12/15/opinion/sunday/women-architects.html.

2. At the time of this writing, that decade has been surpassed, and it's likely to take another decade.

3. Also referred to by terms such as "interim use," "meanwhile use," "tactical urbanism," and "creative placemaking."

4. "Park(ing) Day," Park(ing) Day, accessed December 11, 2022, https:// www.myparkingday.org/.

5. New York City Department of Transportation (NYC DOT), "NYC Plaza Program," accessed December 11, 2022, https://www.nyc.gov/html/dot /html/pedestrians/nyc-plaza-program.shtml.

6. Jesse Hirsch and Reyhan Harmanci, "A Few Temporary Stores or a Neighborhood," *New York Times*, December 2, 2011, accessed December 11, 2022, https://www.nytimes.com/2011/12/02/us/popuphood-opens-temporary-store-neighborhood-in-oakland.html.

7. Edward W. Soja, *Seeking Spatial Justice* (Minneapolis: University of Minnesota Press, 2010).

8. Dara Kerr, "Uber, Lyft IPOs to Mint Next Batch of Bay Area Millionaires," CNET, December 24, 2018, accessed February 1, 2022, https:// www.cnet.com/culture/uber-lyft-ipos-to-mint-next-batch-of-bay-area -millionaires/.

9. City and County of San Francisco, Office of Economic and Workforce Development, "Appendix F: Socioeconomic Neighborhood Profiles," February 2021, accessed February 1, 2022, https://oewd.org/sites/default /files/Documents/Bid%20Opportunities/RFP%20122%20-%20Appen dix%20F%20-%20Socioeconomic%20Neighborhood%20Profiles.pdf.

10. Nishat Awan, Tatjana Schneider, and Jeremy Till, "Introduction," in

Spatial Agency: Other Ways of Doing Architecture (London: Routledge, 2011), 32.

11. I want to acknowledge that "citizen" can be a problematic term when it comes to articulating rights and agency considering legacies of colonialism, capitalism, and White supremacy. But my interpretation of its use in the book is in the context of an individual who is an inhabitant of or has a relationship with a place.

12. Brené Brown, "The Power of Vulnerability," filmed in 2010 in Houston, Texas, TEDx video, 20:03, accessed December 11, 2022, https://www .ted.com/talks/brene_brown_the_power_of_vulnerability.

13. "NOW Hunters Point Project Report, 2014–2016," http://intentional shift.org/wp-content/uploads/2017/12/NHP_Report_20171019_online .pdf.

14. nayyirah waheed, Goodreads, accessed December 13, 2022, https://www .goodreads.com/quotes/9667606-anger-is-often-grief-that-has-been-silent -for-too.

15. Chris Johnson, *Question Bridge*, Question Bridge, accessed December 13, 2022, http://questionbridge.com/.

16. Ida Mojadad, "Walking the Fine Line between Art as a Community Anchor or Fueler of Gentrification," Next City, October 11, 2019, accessed December 13, 2022, https://nextcity.org/daily/entry/walking -the-fine-line-between-community-anchor-or-fueler-of-gentrification.

17. Seyma Bayram, "The Failed Akron Innerbelt Drove Decades of Racial Inequity. Can the Damage Be Repaired?," *Akron (OH) Beacon Journal*, February 3, 2022, accessed December 13, 2022, https://www.beacon journal.com/in-depth/news/2022/02/03/akron-innerbelt-history-racial -inequity-black-history-urban-renewal-ohio/9033520002/.

18. Ascala Sisk et al., "Confronting Power and Privilege for Inclusive, Equitable, and Healthy Communities," *British Medical Journal* (blog), April 16, 2020, accessed December 13, 2022, https://blogs.bmj.com/bmj/2020 /04/16/confronting-power-and-privilege-for-inclusive-equitable-and -healthy-communities/.

19. If you're interested in learning more about how to understand and process different types of grief as well as some of the resources available to do so, What's Your Grief (https://whatsyourgrief.com/) and Modern Loss (https://modernloss.com/) are two great places to start your journey.

Chapter 3. Unseen Dimensions of Public Space: Disrupting Colonial Narratives

1. Thomas W. Cowger, *The National Congress of American Indians: The Founding Years* (Lincoln: University of Nebraska Press, 1999), 13.

2. "Monuments in Perspective" by Erin Genia, MIT School of Architecture and Planning, April 2019, https://act.mit.edu/2019/04/monuments-in-perspective-by-erin-genia/.

3. Confluence Project, "What Is Confluence?," http://www.confluenceproject.org/about/.

4. Toma Villa, *She Who Watches*, Confluence Project, June 28, 2019, http://www.confluenceproject.org/library-post/she-who-watches-by-toma-villa-short-version/.

5. Craig Fortier, *Unsettling the Commons: Social Movements Within, Against, and Beyond Settler Colonialism* (Winnipeg, Manitoba: ARP, 2017).

Chapter 4. Renewing Spatial Agency for a Community: The Freedom Center, Oklahoma City

1. Freedom Center of Oklahoma City, "Who We Are," accessed May 20, 2023, https://freedomcenterokc.org/.

Chapter 5. The Harriet Tubman Memorial, Newark

1. Rebecca Panico, NJ Advance Media for NJ.com, "Another Christopher Columbus Statue Removed from N.J. City Park," NJ.com, June 26, 2020, updated June 27, 2020, accessed January 5, 2023, https://www.nj.com/essex/2020/06/another-christopher-columbus-statue-removed-from-nj-city-park.html.

2. Niall Atkinson, Ann Liu, and Mimi Zeiger, "On Dimensions of Citizenship," in *Dimensions of Citizenship: Architecture and Belonging from the Body to the Cosmos*, publication from the 16th International Architecture Exhibition of the Venice Biennale, 2018, http://dimensionsofcitizenship.org/essays/on-dimensions-of-citizenship/index.html.

3. Sampada Aranke, "Material Matters: Black Radical Aesthetics and the Limits of Visibility," *e-flux Journal*, no. 79 (February 2017), https://www.e-flux.com/journal/79/94433/material-matters-black-radical-aesthetics-and-the-limits-of-visibility/.

4. Monument Lab, "National Monument Audit: Key Findings," 2021, accessed January 7, 2023, https://monumentlab.com/audit.

5. Harry Blain, "The Dangers of Political Sainthood," openDemocracy, October 1, 2017, accessed January 8, 2023, https://www.opendemocracy.net/en/transformation/dangers-of-political-sainthood/.

6. Blain, "Dangers of Political Sainthood."

7. Four Corners Public Arts, *Will You Be My Monument*, 2021, accessed January 7, 2023, https://www.fourcornerspublicarts.org/willyoubemymonument.

8. Colleen O'Dea, "Newark before the Comeback: A City Marked by White Flight, Poor Policy," NJ Spotlight News, September 4, 2019, accessed January 6, 2023, https://www.njspotlightnews.org/2019/09/19-09-02-newark-before-the-comeback-a-city-marked-by-white-flight-and-poor-policy/.

9. O'Dea, "Newark before the Comeback."

10. Mellon Foundation, "Humanities in Place," https://mellon.org/programs/humanities-place/.

11. From a concept presentation video by Nina Cooke John.

12. Sarah H. Bradford, *Scenes in the Life of Harriet Tubman* (n.p.: Andesite Press, 2015).

13. Kate Clifford Larson, *Bound for the Promised Land: Harriet Tubman; Portrait of an American Hero* (New York: One World/Ballantine, 2005), 100.

14. Robert Hayden, "Runagate Runagate," Poetry Foundation, https://www.poetryfoundation.org/poems/52947/runagate-runagate.

Chapter 6. Materializing Memory: The Camp Barker Memorial in Washington, DC

1. Arthur C. Danto, "The Vietnam Veterans Memorial," *Nation* 241 (August 31, 1985): 152.

2. Booth Gunter, Jamie Kizzire, and Cindy Kent, "Whose Heritage? Public Symbols of the Confederacy," Southern Poverty Law Center, 14–15, https://www.splcenter.org/sites/default/files/com_whose_heritage.pdf.

3. "Memorial Carving," Stone Mountain Park, https://www.stonemountainpark.com/activities/history-nature/confederate-memorial-carving/.

4. Martin Luther King Jr., "I Have a Dream," Lincoln Memorial, Washington, DC, August 28, 1963.

5. "Memorial Carving."

6. Stone Mountain Memorial Association, "History of Stone Mountain Memorial Association," http://stonemountainpark.org/about-us/history-of-smma/.

7. "The Legal Support for Park Changes," Stone Mountain Action Coalition, https://stonemountainaction.org/legal.

8. Timothy Pratt and Rick Rojas, "Giant Confederate Monument Will Remain at Revamped Stone Mountain," *New York Times*, May 24, 2021, https://www.nytimes.com/2021/05/24/us/stone-mountain-confederate-monument-georgia.html.

9. Chandra Manning, "Contraband Camps and the African American Refugee Experience during the Civil War," *Oxford Research Encyclopedia of American History*, December 19, 2017, accessed January 20, 2023, https://doi.org/10.1093/acrefore/9780199329175.013.203.

10. "Camp Barker," *Evening Star*, October 24, 1862.

11. "Camp Barker."

12. Robert Harrison, *Washington during Civil War and Reconstruction: Race and Radicalism* (Cambridge: Cambridge University Press, 2011), 41.

13. Joseph P. Reidy, "'Coming from the Shadow of the Past': The Transition from Slavery to Freedom at Freedmen's Village, 1863–1900," *Virginia Magazine of History and Biography* 95, no. 4 (October 1987): 403–428.

14. Chris Myers Asch and George Derek Musgrove, *Chocolate City: A History of Race and Democracy in the Nation's Capital* (Chapel Hill: University of North Carolina Press, 2017), 123–128; Matthew Pinsker, *Lincoln's Sanctuary: Abraham Lincoln and the Soldiers' Home* (Oxford: Oxford University Press, 2003), 68.

15. Washington, DC, Department of General Services, "Percent for Art," https://dgs.dc.gov/page/percent-art.

16. For more discussion of the memorial's reception and relationship to events beyond Camp Barker, specifically gun violence in American schools, see Sharine Taylor, "The Camp Barker Memorial Is a Sobering Look at America's Past (and Present)," *Azure*, August 19, 2019, https://www.azuremagazine.com/article/the-camp-barker-memorial-is-a-sobering-look-at-americas-past-and-present/.

17. Renée Ater, "Contemporary Monuments to the Slave Past," https://www
.slaverymonuments.org/.

Chapter 7. Practicing _mpathic design: The Charlottesville Memorial for Peace and Justice

1. Susan Lanzoni, *Empathy: A History* (New Haven, CT: Yale University Press, 2018), 2.

2. Lanzoni, *Empathy*, 2.

3. Lanzoni, *Empathy*, 2.

4. Mabel O. Wilson, *Begin with the Past: Building the National Museum of African American History and Culture* (Washington, DC: Smithsonian Books, 2016), 10.

5. Equal Justice Initiative (EJI), "Community Remembrance Project," accessed November 24, 2021, https://eji.org/projects/community-remem brance-project/.

6. EJI, "Community Remembrance Project."

7. Albemarle County, Virginia, County Executive, Office of Equity and Inclusion, "Community Remembrance Project," accessed October 21, 2019, https://www.albemarle.org/government/county-executive/office-of -equity-inclusion/community-remembrance.

8. Brendan Wolfe, "The Train at Wood's Crossing," accessed January 19, 2022, http://brendanwolfe.com/lynching.

9. Brendan Wolfe, "The Lynching of John Henry James (1898)," *Encyclo- pedia Virginia/Virginia Humanities*, accessed December 2, 2019, https:// encyclopediavirginia.org/entries/lynching-of-john-henry-james-1898-the/.

10. Andrea Douglas and Jalane Schmidt, "Marked by These Monuments," accessed December 15, 2022, https://www.thesemonuments.org.

11. Andrew Katz, ed., "Unrest in Virginia: Clashes over a Show of White Nationalism in Charlottesville Turn Deadly," *Time* photo-essay, accessed January 28, 2023, https://time.com/charlottesville-white-nationalist -rally-clashes/.

12. Derrick Bryson Taylor, "Confederate Statue Near Site of White National- ist Rally in Charlottesville Is Removed," *New York Times*, September 12, 2020, https://www.nytimes.com/2020/09/12/us/charlottesville-confeder ate-statue-at-ready.html.

13. Hawes Spencer and Michael Levenson, "Charlottesville Removes Robert E. Lee Statue at Center of White Nationalist Rally," *New York Times*, July 9, 2021, updated November 8, 2021, https://www.nytimes.com/2021 /07/09/us/charlottesville-confederate-monuments-lee.html.

14. Albemarle County, Virginia, County Executive, Communications and Public Engagement, "Court Square," accessed December 17, 2022, https://www.albemarle.org/government/county-executive/communi cations-public-engagement/let-s-talk-albemarle/court-square.

15. Tricia Hersey, *Rest Is Resistance: A Manifesto* (New York: Little, Brown Spark, 2022), 83, 161.

16. Hersey, *Rest Is Resistance*, 187.

17. LaToya Baldwin Clark, "We Are Not Our Ancestors' Wildest Dreams. We Are Our Ancestors," Medium, February 8, 2021, https://lbaldwin clark.medium.com/we-are-not-our-ancestors-wildest-dreams-we-are-our -ancestors-b8123ae8854b.

18. Cvillepedia, "Court Square Park," accessed January 29, 2023, https:// www.cvillepedia.org/Court_Square_Park.

19. Albemare County, Virginia, "Court Square," accessed September 2, 2022.

20. Albemarle County, Virginia, City of Charlottesville, "Historic Court Square," accessed November 26, 2019, https://www.charlottesville.org /departments-and-services/departments-h-z/neighborhood-development -services/historic-preservation-and-design-review/historic-resources -committee/local-markers/historic-court-square. The Stonewall Jackson statue in Court Square is one of three (including the Robert E. Lee statue a few blocks west) donated by local philanthropist Paul Goodloe McIntire as part of Charlottesville's City Beautiful movement. A review of Daniel Bluestone's research of Court Square is a prerequisite for historical and spatial understanding of Court Square. Daniel Bluestone, *Buildings, Landscapes, and Memory: Case Studies in Historic Preservation* (New York: W. W. Norton, 2011), 222–230.

21. The actions of the Charlottesville KKK are well documented: Citizen Justice Initiative, "The Illusion of Progress: Charlottesville's Roots in White Supremacy," Carter G. Woodson Institute, 2017, https://uvalibrary.maps .arcgis.com/apps/Cascade/index.html?appid=3e111d602453478cad8452 ba551138b6.

22. Daniel Bluestone, *Buildings, Landscapes, and Memory*, 222–230.

Chapter 8. Incorporating Empathy: *To Middle Species, With Love,* Columbus, Indiana

1. Thomas Nagel, "What Is It Like to Be a Bat?" *Philosophical Review* 83, no. 4 (October 1974): 435–450, https://doi.org/10.2307/2183914.

2. Jakob von Uexküll, *A Foray into the Worlds of Animals and Humans* (originally published in German in 1934), trans. Joseph D. O'Neil (Minneapolis: University of Minnesota Press, 2010).

3. Landmark Columbus Foundation, Exhibit Columbus, *Public by Design*, https://www.exhibitcolumbus.org/.

4. "New Middles" was the theme for the 2020–2021 cycle of Exhibit Columbus, curated and developed by Mimi Zeiger and Iker Gil.

5. Mill Race Park: landscape architect is Michael Van Valkenburgh; architect is Stanley Saitowitz.

6. Julia P. S. Hoeh et al., "In Artificial Roost Comparison, Bats Show Preference for Rocket Box Style," *PLoS ONE* 13, no. 10 (October 31, 2018): e0205701, https://doi.org/10.1371/journal.pone.0205701.

7. Grayson Haver Currin, "Vilified for Virus, Bats Are a New Album's Seductive Stars," *New York Times*, June 10, 2020, https://www.nytimes.com/2020/06/10/arts/music/bats-field-works-ultrasonic.html.

8. Shawn Chiki and Onokio, *To Middle Species, With Love*, digital album, Bandcamp, https://tomiddlespecieswithlove.bandcamp.com/album/to-middle-species-with-love.

Chapter 9. Teaching Empathic Community Engagement Using Storytelling

1. bell hooks, *Teaching to Transgress: Education as the Practice of Freedom* (New York: Routledge, 2014).

2. Carnegie Foundation Elective Classifications, "The Elective Classification for Community Engagement," September 30, 2022, https://carnegieelectiveclassifications.org/the-2024-elective-classification-for-community-engagement/#:~:text=Community%20engagement%20describes%20collaboration%20between,context%20of%20partnership%20and%20reciprocity.

3. Chris R. Glass and Hiram E. Fitzgerald, "Engaged Scholarship: Historical Roots, Contemporary Challenges," in *Handbook of Engaged Scholarship: Contemporary Landscapes, Future Directions*, vol. 1, *Institutional Change,*

ed. Hiram E. Fitzgerald, Cathy Burack, and Sarena D. Seifer (East Lansing: Michigan State University Press, 2010), 9–24.

4. Kellogg Commission on the Future of State and Land-Grant Institutions, "Returning to Our Roots: The Engaged Institution," February 1999, https://www.aplu.org/wp-content/uploads/returning-to-our-roots-the -engaged-institution.pdf.

5. Jennifer Furze et al., "Student Perceptions of a Community Engagement Experience: Exploration of Reflections on Social Responsibility and Professional Formation," *Physiotherapy Theory and Practice* 27, no. 6 (2011): 411–421, https://doi.org/10.3109/09593985.2010.516479.

6. John Dewey, "Experience and Education," *Educational Forum* 50, no. 3 (1986): 241–252, https://doi.org/10.1080/00131728609335764.

7. John Dewey, *How We Think* (n.p.: DigiCat, 2022).

8. Dewey, "Experience and Education."

9. Dewey, "Experience and Education."

10. Donald A. Schön, *The Reflective Practitioner: How Professionals Think in Action* (New York: Basic Books, 1984).

11. Schön, *Reflective Practitioner.*

12. David A. Kolb, *Experiential Learning: Experience as the Source of Learning and Development* (Upper Saddle River, NJ: Prentice Hall, 1984).

13. Kolb, *Experiential Learning.*

14. Leonie Sandercock, *Cosmopolis II: Mongrel Cities of the 21st Century* (London: Continuum, 2003).

15. Sandercock, *Cosmopolis II.*

16. Patsy Healey, "Relational Complexity and the Imaginative Power of Strategic Spatial Planning," *European Planning Studies* 14, no. 4 (2006): 525–546, https://doi.org/10.1080/09654310500421196.

17. Judith E. Innes and David E. Booher, *Planning with Complexity: An Introduction to Collaborative Rationality for Public Policy*, 2nd ed. (New York: Routledge, 2018).

18. Leonie Sandercock, ed., *Making the Invisible Visible: A Multicultural Planning History* (Berkeley: University of California Press, 1998).

19. Lynn Abrams, *Oral History Theory*, 2nd ed. (London: Routledge, 2016).

20. Abrams, *Oral History Theory.*

21. Schön, *Reflective Practitioner*.

Afterword. Planning with Purpose: Repairing Past Harm with Empathy

1. Mitchell J. Silver, "Anatomy and Soul of a Place," in *Local Planning: Contemporary Principles and Practice*, ed. Gary Hack et al. (Washington, DC: ICMA Press, 2009), 61–65.

2. American Planning Association, "AICP Code of Ethics and Professional Conduct," adopted March 19, 2005; effective June 1, 2005; revised April 1, 2016, and November 2021; https://www.planning.org/ethics/ethicscode/.

3. American Planning Association, "AICP Code of Ethics."

4. Harriet Bogdanowicz, "Planning Directors Issue Racial Equity Statement and Call to Action," American Planning Association, blog post, September 29, 2021, https://www.planning.org/blog/9221218/planning-directors-issue-racial-equity-statement-and-call-to-action/.

5. Mitchell J. Silver, "Lead and Inspire with Purpose: AICP Code of Ethics Update," American Planning Association, blog post, January 2022, https://www.planning.org/blog/9227093/lead-and-inspire-with-purpose-aicp-code-of-ethics-update/.

6. Jacquelyne Germain, "The Fight for Reparations Has Stalled in Congress. Here's What They Look Like in State and Local Governments," CNN, July 13, 2022, https://www.cnn.com/2022/07/13/us/reparations-state-local-commission-reaj/index.html.

7. Janie Har, "San Francisco Board Open to Reparations with $5M Payouts," Associated Press, March 15, 2023, https://apnews.com/article/san-francisco-black-reparations-5-million-36899f7974c751950a8ce0e444f86189.

8. New York City Department of Parks and Recreation, "Cadman Plaza Park: Juneteenth Grove," https://www.nycgovparks.org/parks/cadman-plaza-park-and-brooklyn-war-memorial/highlights/19868.

About the Editor

Photo credit: Sneha Patel

Elgin Cleckley, NOMA, is an assistant professor of architecture and design at the University of Virginia (UVA) with an appointment in the School of Education and Human Development and the School of Nursing. He is the director of design justice at UVA's Equity Center (Democracy Initiative Center for the Redress of Inequity Through Community-Engaged Scholarship).

He is the principal of _mpathic design, an internationally recognized, multi-award-winning pedagogy, initiative, and professional practice. Elgin has worked in professional practice at offices in Seattle, New York, Chicago, and Toronto.

Elgin is a recipient of UVA's Alumni Board of Trustees Teaching Award (the highest teaching award an assistant professor can receive at the university), UVA's Distinguished Public Scholar Award, and the Armstead Robinson Faculty Award. He has received three Association of

Collegiate Schools of Architecture Awards—for Creative Achievement (for an _mpathic design advanced studio), Diversity Achievement, and Faculty Design (Honorable Mention). He was nominated for a State Council of Higher Education for Virginia Outstanding Faculty Award and received a US Department of Education Blue Ribbon Award, Campus Compact Virginia's Community Engagement Award, and an AIA Virginia Award. His scholarship received a Dumbarton Oaks Mellon Fellowship in Urban Landscape Studies / Harvard University. Elgin's scholarship is a recipient of fellowships from MacDowell, Loghaven, Anderson Center, Good Hart, and Art Omi.

About the Contributors

C.L. Bohannon is associate professor of landscape architecture and associate dean of justice, equity, diversity, and inclusion at the University of Virginia. Bohannon is a nationally recognized scholar and educator in the areas of community-engaged design and pedagogy, social and environmental justice, and African American landscapes, especially in the American South.

Elgin Cleckley is an assistant professor of architecture and design with an appointment in the School of Education and Human Development and the School of Nursing at the University of Virginia. He is the principal of _mpathic design, an internationally recognized, multi-award-winning pedagogy, initiative, and professional practice. Elgin is a recipient of three Association of Collegiate Schools of Architecture Awards, an Alumni Board of Trustees Teaching Award, and

UVA's Distinguished Public Scholar Award, and he has been awarded fellowships at Dumbarton Oaks, Loghaven, MacDowell, Art Omi, Good Hart, and Anderson Center at Tower View. He is the director of design justice at UVA's Equity Center (Democracy Initiative Center for the Redress of Inequity Through Community-Engaged Scholarship), where he leads the school's NOMA Project Pipeline: Architecture Mentorship Program.

Nina Cooke John is the founding principal of Studio Cooke John Architecture and Design, a multidisciplinary design studio that values place-making as a way to transform relationships between people and the built environment. The studio was awarded a 2021 AIA Merit Award for the public art installation *Point of Action*, commissioned for the Flatiron Public Plazas in 2020. Cooke John was named a 2022 United States Artists Fellow. Her work has also been featured in *Architectural Record*, *Madame Architect*, the *New York Times*, *Dwell*, NBC's *Open House*, the AIA Center for Architecture's 2018 exhibition *Close to the Edge: The Birth of Hip-Hop Architecture*, and PBS *NewsHour Weekend*.

Christine Gaspar is a designer and planner with over fifteen years of experience in community-engaged design practice. From 2009 to 2022, she was executive director of the Center for Urban Pedagogy (CUP), a New York–based nonprofit whose mission is to use the power of design and art to increase meaningful civic engagement in partnership with historically marginalized communities. Prior to that, she was assistant director of the Gulf Coast Community Design Studio in Biloxi, Mississippi. She is a founding member of the Design Futures Student Leadership Forum Advisory Board.

Erin Genia is an enrolled member of the Sisseton-Wahpeton Oyate. She is a multidisciplinary artist, educator, and community organizer specializing in Native American and Indigenous arts and culture. Genia's artistic practice merges Dakota cultural imperatives, pure expression, and exploration of materiality with the conceptual. Her work has received attention from diverse audiences and has been exhibited nationally and internationally at the Urbano Project in Boston, the Venice Biennale, Ars Electronica, and the International Space Station.

Cory Henry is the principal of the award-winning Los Angeles–based namesake Atelier Cory Henry. His work ranges in scale and type, operating in the fields of architecture, urban design, new media art, installations, and public space design. Atelier Cory Henry's projects span several continents. Henry is a fellow of the Royal Society of Arts (United Kingdom), has been recognized by the National Council of Architectural Registration Boards (NCARB) as an emerging force in design and architecture, and won the US National Emerging Architect On Olive contemporary housing competition. He has twice been named KEA Distinguished Professor by the University of Maryland School of Architecture, Planning and Preservation.

Joyce Hwang is associate professor of architecture at the University at Buffalo SUNY and founder of Ants of the Prairie. She is a recipient of the Exhibit Columbus University Design Research Fellowship, the Architectural League Emerging Voices Award, the New York Foundation for the Arts (NYFA) Fellowship, the New York State Council on the Arts (NYSCA) Independent Project Grant, and the MacDowell Fellowship. Her work has been featured by the Museum of Modern Art and exhibited at the Brooklyn Botanic Garden, Matadero Madrid, the Venice Architecture Biennale, and the International Architecture Biennale Rotterdam, among other venues. Hwang is a registered architect in New York State and has practiced professionally with offices in New York, Philadelphia, San Francisco, and Barcelona.

Katie MacDonald is cofounder of After Architecture, director of the Before Building Laboratory, and assistant professor of architecture at the University of Virginia. MacDonald's work advances circular construction materials. She engages emerging technologies to work with natural materials and processes in new ways, reframing the relationship between biology, technology, and authorship. Recent accolades include *Architect Magazine*'s Research + Development Award and two Best of Design Awards from *The Architect's Newspaper* in the Research and Digital Fabrication categories.

Liz Ogbu is a designer, urbanist, and spatial justice activist. Ogbu is an expert on engaging and transforming unjust urban environments. Her multidisciplinary design practice, Studio O, operates at the intersection of racial and spatial justice. She collaborates with/in communities in need to leverage design to address collective harm and catalyze community healing. Her honors include IDEO.org Global Fellow, Aspen Ideas Scholar, LISC Rubinger Fellow, and TEDWomen Speaker.

Kyle Schumann is cofounder of After Architecture, director of the Before Building Laboratory, and assistant professor of architecture at the University of Virginia. Schumann's work advances circular construction technologies. Schumann seeks to increase the accessibility of computation and robotic construction, leveraging democratized and consumer-grade technologies and inventing and building low-cost ground-up construction systems. Recent accolades include *Architect Magazine*'s Research + Development Award and two Best of Design Awards from *The Architect's Newspaper* in the Research and Digital Fabrication categories.

Mitchell J. Silver is a principal with McAdams, a land planning and design company. He is responsible for providing advisory services in urban planning and in parks and public space planning. He is an award-winning planner with more than thirty-eight years of experience and is internationally recognized for his leadership and contributions to contemporary planning issues. He is a prolific public speaker, and he specializes in comprehensive planning, place-making, and implementation strategies. Prior to joining McAdams, Mitchell served as commissioner for the New York City Department of Parks and Recreation; chief planning officer for Raleigh, North Carolina; and president of the American Planning Association and the American Institute of Certified Planners.

Index